#BRokenPromises, Black Deaths, & Blue Ribbons

Transgressions: Cultural Studies and Education

VOLUME 128

The titles published in this series are listed at *brill.com/tcse*

#BRokenPromises, Black Deaths, & Blue Ribbons

Understanding, Complicating, and Transcending Police-Community Violence

Edited by

Kenneth J. Fasching-Varner, Kerri J. Tobin and
Stephen M. Lentz

BRILL

SENSE

LEIDEN | BOSTON

All chapters in this book have undergone peer review.

The Library of Congress Cataloging-in-Publication Data is available online at
http://catalog.loc.gov

ISSN 2214-9732
ISBN 978-90-04-37871-1 (paperback)
ISBN 978-90-04-37872-8 (hardback)
ISBN 978-90-04-37873-5 (e-book)

This book is printed on acid-free paper and produced in a sustainable manner.

CONTENTS

CONTENTS

KENNETH J. FASCHING-VARNER, KERRI J. TOBIN
AND STEPHEN M. LENTZ

BLACK BODIES, BLUE RIBBONS

An Introduction

Summer 2016 may go down in history as one of the most volatile seasons in the history of Baton Rouge, Louisiana. From the killing of Alton Sterling to the assassination of three law enforcement officers and a 1000-year flood, the spirit of Baton Rouge was tested in unprecedented ways. The resilience of people of Baton Rouge led many to share the hashtag #unBRoken on social media, but the hashtag was, in many ways, deceiving. Baton Rouge, like many urban centres throughout the United States and beyond, has always had at its core racial, class, and other divides.

As editors of this book, and faculty members at Louisiana State University and Baton Rouge Community College, we were geographically located in the middle of the complex events of that summer, but they are, lamentably, not unique. Before and after summer 2016 we see in Kodachrome-like colour tensions at many levels that make moving forward difficult; tensions between law enforcement and communities of colour are but one manifestation of larger racial and class divides that permeate the fabric of our society.

THE EVOLUTION OF THIS BOOK

This book was contracted, initially, with Rowman and Littlefield, to be published in 2017, concurrent with President Trump's first year in office and about a year after the events of the Summer of 2016. In early fall of 2016, after proposing the book and having the proposal peer reviewed by experts in the field, we negotiated a contract with Rowman and Littlefield to publish this text. Soon after that contract was issued, Rowman and Littlefield parted ways with the acquisition editor who brought the title to contract and Thomas F. Koerner, the Vice President and Publisher for Education, took over the project. From the moment that Mr. Koerner came on board, a divide opened between the vision we had as editors and the politically conservative approach that Mr. Koerner takes to publishing. In an email on January 2, 2017 Mr. Koerner wrote, in part,

> You mention the "discourses from the alt-right that serve to further complicate the already existing divides that rip through the core of many urban centers." I prefer an objective presentation that does not politicize the

situation, hoping to see activities on both the right and left that have exacerbated the situation.

In response, one of the editors wrote back to Mr. Koerner on January 4, 2017, asserting, in part,

> Well there really is no such thing as an objective presentation, though we are comfortable holding right and left accountable. Alt-right is not necessarily a variation or proxy for right just as neo-liberal is not a variation of left or liberal. I think the larger issue is white nationalism and racism that has manifest in a particular way at the end of the Obama era – an era that many wanted to suggest was post-racial. Now that we have a president elect this will also intensify the conversation and the book would come out timely to the first quarter of the Trump 1st term. The situation, is, however a political one as the entire spectrum of political standpoints influences how these issues have played out. We agree though that the entire spectrum is up for critique and is fair game to be analyzed within the context of this text. I think the concept of alt-right, which in many ways is a sanitized way of discussing white nationalism, has to be discussed given the myriad ways in which urban centers are being attacked from forces within and outside. We will treat this concern fairly (not claiming objectivity).

Mr. Koerner wrote back the next day, in part,

> I appreciate your thoughtful responses, which I need to mull over a bit, especially "fair" vs. "objective." If it appears that "white nationalism" is described exclusively as a conservative issue, I will take issue with it.

In response, one of the editors responded to Mr. Koerner, the same day, January 5th, and wrote:

> Hi Tom,
>
> If you look at my response carefully I think I clearly said those issues are issues across the political spectrum and reflect a tension of the end of the Obama era which had been lauded as post racial and our current moment which is clearly racialized. [We] have considerable expertise with this subject and if we cannot have a direct and open conversation in a text that is trying to get at the heart of the problem then we would be exacerbating the problem. This topic is timely and as such we are ready to move forward – if you want to great and if not that is fine too, we just need to know.

At this point, the editorial team made it clear whether or not Rowman and Littlefield wanted to publish the book was less relevant, but what was clear was our commitment to the particular direction of the book and commitment to not whitewashing the content of this book. Mr. Koerner, for his part, wrote back on the 5th of January and said "… I agree the subject is red-hot. Please proceed."

We did proceed, and in the end procured 30 chapters that represent a variety of perspectives and viewpoints aimed at addressing the concerns of communities of colour, including but not limited to police violence. After submitting the manuscript, we heard no word from Rowman and Littlefield for several weeks. On October 4, 2017, Mr. Koerner wrote, in part,

> As alluded to in earlier e-mails, I remain very concerned about the focus (and tone) of many of the contributed chapters in that they reflect one side of the proverbial coin. Very political at this time! Basically, I don't believe our readers want a sermon from those who admittedly represent one side. Rather they want to read thoughtful solutions, not the liberal slant that's so prevalent among those in higher education. The readership of your book is likely to be broad, but all interested in what can be done.

At that point, we reminded Mr. Koerner in a telephone call that *everything* is political and that his conceptualization of "liberal slant" and not wanting "a sermon" from the authors was revealing – not only one of the major roadblocks to progress on these issues in general, but also in how it paralleled an urge to censor authors in a way that President Trump has worked to try to limit the role of media in confronting hard truths. We did agree to reformat certain sections of the book and add some discourse to the introduction to address his concerns, but we communicated as we had in January that our commitment was to honoring the truths of these authors, and that in fact an audience interested in an academic book on this subject was likely not looking for an approach that justified violence against communities of color in an attempt to be "fair" to white supremacists, xenophobes, and the like. Delays in communication persisted, as did a newly-invented need to have the book re-reviewed by outside readers. Ultimately, Mr. Koerner wrote back saying

> …what continues to be problematic is a snide statement in the Introduction about President Trump's reaction in the wake of Hurricane Harvey. That kind of approach, entirely subjective, is divisive and does little to heal the present state of affairs. And, if the book's purpose is to show what and how must be done (especially by schools and educators), as I mentioned earlier, some of the chapters do just the opposite in sermonizing about race relations.

From our perspective, we were confused by the editor's persistent desire to censor the authors and neutralize the realities that they speak to, as many academics, community members, and religious leaders know to be true and persistent.

Our commitment to discussing race is a primary focus of the book and the chapters in this book outline what is are real issues regarding violence targeted against communities of color. The way to address issues of violence that are racialized is not by walking away from that discussion within the text. And the idea that such a discussion is sermonizing along with the suggestion that chapters are "very political" and represent a "liberal slant" reveals a significant bias on the part of the publisher.

It is alarmingly also consistent with how the alt-right and far-right have attempted to walk away from responsibility for the increased white nationalistic violence in the United States since the candidacy and presidency of Donald Trump.

Given that it was clear Rowman and Littlefield had no interest in honoring the contract and agreement, despite our having exhaustively discussed our concerns and commitments early and throughout the process, we approached Shirley Steinberg, a series editor, about bringing the completed manuscript to Brill | Sense. Shirley shared our concerns about the attempt at neutralizing the critique based on race and the reality that many communities of color experience. As a result, we decided to move the manuscript to Brill | Sense so that we could honor the work and commitment of the authors, which is consistent with how this project was conceived, proposed, and engaged.

We felt it was important to the reader that we outline this history before diving into the specifics of the manuscript.

THE CONTEXT

A common link between communities (particularly communities of colour) and law enforcement is a mistrust that seems to have expanded, at least in the overall public consciousness, in recent decades, with violence against communities of colour (both physical and psychological), and the appearance of a seeming disinvestment in urban centres. The problem is not new by any means; rather, it is reflective of an historical trend.

What we have seen is a sharp rise in public white nationalistic discourses, from the so-called "alt-right," that had always existed slightly below the surface. We also see, in many ways, a complicated apathy and fatigue from a largely disengaged electorate, and a neo-liberal core economic orientation, working in concert to further complicate the already existing divides that rip through many urban centres.

Vows to unite communities and bridge differences that many leaders at local and (inter)national levels have articulated seem to be broken promises. In the wake of the #unBRoken hashtag campaign, we cannot help but see "unbroken" as diametrically opposed to the reality here. To make sense of the seemingly incomprehensible set of circumstances, people have used many means to communicate about these issues: faith groups, social media, and localized organizations are some of these avenues. But despite our means and mechanisms, bringing the myriad and multiplicity of voices together to think through the meanings of these events and contemplating our pathways forward seems largely absent.

In the wake of Hurricane Harvey, we saw the United States President more focused on crowd size and congratulating his own presence than dealing with the conditions (in this case, both infrastructure and community organization) that intensified the devastation. It was hard to see much of an affective or emotional engagement with communities suffering the most. We see a daily barrage of separation, along lines of race, class, sexuality, and other identities that do not just come from the White

House but seem also to come from 'our houses' – the very communities affected by human interaction.

The fundamental premise of this book, however, is that until various interest holders come together to reflect on the big questions that remain unanswered, and do so in a way that brings the multitude of perspectives together, the promise of a prosperous and engaged citizenry will remain significantly broken. As a result, we asked authors to think through some of the complexities, realities, and pathways forward. Five questions that flowed through our collective effort were:

1. *First, what factors contribute to the creation of divided cities and communities, particularly along lines of race and class?* Many urban centers appear to tell tales of division going far back in history. Citizen within dominant-culture communities used resources and created segregated living, schooling, and socializing, while non-dominant groups suffered in poor living conditions created by that segregation. We asked ourselves and contributors to this volume to consider and contemplate what, from their vantage points and perspectives, led to this phenomenon.

2. *Second, what does the landscape look like today?* Contributors to this section offer portraits and cross-sections of the housing, schooling, and policing profiles of some major urban areas of the country. Who lives where, how is money shared among citizens, and what demographics help us gain insight into our divided society?

3. *Third, what types of experiences are emblematic of our divided relationships?* Here we asked contributors to share their own personal run-ins with law enforcement, time spent protesting or deciding whether to participate in collective action, as well as to reflect on how racial divisions are evident within their own communities. They focus on factors, conditions, and experiences leading to dichotomized perspectives about law enforcement in particular and community dynamics more generally.

4. *Fourth, what roles do schools play in the maintenance of our segregated cities, and in the mistrust that permeates relationships between law enforcement and communities of color?* Our cities grapple with segregation not only in housing and community representation, but also at school. We asked contributors in this section to think about how these divided schools have come to be, how are they maintained, and what role schools play in defining relationships between students, families, and law enforcement.

5. *Finally, and more broadly, whose lives really matter, and how do we move forward?* We asked contributors to contemplate bigger philosophical issues related to how, and whose, lives matter, as well as what actions we need to take in order to move forward to make our communities more united.

We put out a broad call for chapter proposals and were overwhelmed by over 90 submissions. In the end, we invited 45 contributors to draft full chapters, and ultimately selected these 30 chapters for publication. We ask readers to remember that a volume like this will not, nor should it try to, capture the full complexity of these issues. What we learned is that there are many with perspectives to share, and not enough venues to share musings, thoughts, and intellectual capital. So, we see this volume as a start to what should be many more texts, dialogues, and spaces to contemplate the questions we are asking.

Though by its very design incomplete, this volume is nevertheless important because the disconnects and oft-dysfunctional relationships between law enforcement and the communities they serve are the civil rights challenge of our lifetime. Considerable confusion, anger, frustration, and tension surrounding policing in underrepresented communities have yet to be explored formally through book-length texts. There are no texts that make an attempt to understand the major themes that can lead us to bigger conversation about the nature of reaching toward stronger and more unified communities.

When leaders' articulated commitments do not play out in their actions, communities are left vulnerable and fatigued as the citizens attempt to live their lives and grow in often harsh and hostile environments. The vulnerability and fatigue are exacerbated at the intersections of difference. This volume is important precisely because it provides a space to start conversations, and we invite you to take the themes and discussions in this volume as starting points in concert with your own localized discussions, efforts, and actions toward bringing communities together and moving forward.

In Solidarity,

Kenneth J. Fasching-Varner, Louisiana State University
Kerri J. Tobin, Louisiana State University
Stephen M. Lentz, Baton Rouge Community College

ISSAC CARTER, BEATRIZ GONZALEZ AND CLEVELAND HAYES

1. THE JIM CROW EFFECT ON FEDERAL POLICY AND PRACTICE

Social Engineering and the Making of Metropolis in Black and White

Democracy may be one of the noblest ideas of Western civilization, though the supremacy with respect to the colonial design of race and systems of racism have proven to be more powerful. The United States is built on a hierarchal, polarizing, racial binary of White and Black. From the onset of America's democratic aspiration, racial equity has been absent. It is worthy to note that the first law, ratified after the United States Constitution, was the Naturalization Act of 1790, endorsing free White persons as the only individuals with the capacity for citizenship.

The colored demarcations of America's national resolve are visibly evident in the composition of its cities. The demographics of U.S. towns and neighborhoods are the direct result of deliberate and historical practices of power, privilege, and discrimination. To fully comprehend the scope of this subject commands attention toward the racial tensions after the Civil War.

The Emancipation Proclamation freed enslaved Africans. During Reconstruction, the Thirteenth Amendment abolished slavery, the Fourteenth Amendment addressed citizenship rights of all, and the Fifteenth Amendment prohibited race-based voting discrimination, racism remained a permanent fixture of Americana. Despite those shifts in law, Black citizens were not from anti-Black sentiments and systems. In other words, reconstruction did not universally alter the Nation's mindset regarding race and race relations.

During Reconstruction, White Southerners also enacted a series of laws and ordinances, first known and Slaves Laws and then Black codes, to re-establish the social, political and civil authority of Whites citizens. Within this restrictive system of race-based hate grew the methodologies ultimatley come to known under the moniker of Jim Crow. Whites were legally able to discriminate against the newly freed Black citizens and divide urban America along color lines.

JIM CROW EFFECT

Jim Crow facilitated the oppression of Blacks personally, interpersonally and institutionally in every major societal and cultural structure. The Jim Crow Effect

© KONINKLIJKE BRILL NV, LEIDEN, 2018 | DOI 10.1163/9789004378735_001

created a hostile environment for Black citizens analogous to being an undesired refugee in a foreign country. The relentless targeting of Blacks by Whites proved that after a civil war enemies do not quickly emerge as unified countrymen or countrywomen.

Proliferated by Southern states (though many Northern sentiments aligned), Jim Crow became a way of life throughout the country. The system served as an overarching racial caste system of legalized discrimination. Jim Crow circulated a deficit-based public discourse rationalizing discrimination against Blacks as a natural entitlement bestowed upon White America. The Jim Crow Effect nurtured within the national consciousness the certainty that discrimination against Blacks is necessary and deserved, as their freedom was not.

At the interpersonal and cultural levels, the Jim Crow Effect is evident via race relations, and the prevailing or hegemonic ideology that Whites are superior to Blacks. Jim Crow fuelled beliefs of Black inferiority to Whites through social Darwinism and other pseudo-scientific methods. Jim Crow manufactured fears that Black progress would be at the expense of Whites, and created antagonism at the prospect of forced integration.

The attitudes established an etiquette between White and Black Americans, where Black folks could not shake hands with Whites, or look them Whites directly in the eye, nor interact in the same spaces. The Jim Crow Effect manipulated constitutional laws and ideals to maintain racial segregation. A separate and unequal status quo between Whites and Blacks was firmly established.

Within structural and disciplinary spheres, Jim Crow was also in full effect. Bureaucratic institutions like governmental agencies, banks, and schools all regulated and enforced rules and policies where White leaders exhausted all measures of discrimination to undermine Reconstruction efforts and the break the social contract between the United States and its Black citizens. Blacks, freed after the Civil War, would endure over 100 years of legal, anti-Black discrimination until the 1964 Civil Rights Act, 1965 Voting Act and the 1968 Fair Housing Act.

This near century-long legal discrimination served as the architect of Black and White urban America. The promise of freedom and engagements offered by the ideals of reconstruction has remained elusive within both private and public spheres. The Jim Crow Effect conferred (and maintained) a second-class citizenship status, which affirms America's broken promise.

BROKEN DEALS

Two historical periods – the Great Migration and the Great Depression – provide the historical and social context, to illustrate the Jim Crow Effect in the design of urban America. From the early 1900s through the late 1960s, large masses of Blacks migrated towards Northern and Midwest cities. Driven from their southern roots by unsatisfactory economic opportunities and harsh segregationist laws, Blacks migrated to take advantage of the need for industrial workers during World War I.

2

Still unequal to Whites; industrial work paid substantially more than agricultural work.

After World War I, the 1930s Great Depression, a decade-long period marking the worst economic recession in America's history, saw mass unemployment, bank failures, and the stock market crash. During the Great Depression, Roosevelt implemented a series of social programs to address poverty, unemployment and our nation's damaged financial system, in hopes of preventing another depression, known as the New Deal. The implementation of Roosevelt's social welfare programs suffered from the Jim Crow Effect, disproportionately favouring White America. The Black migrants seeking prosperity in America's metropolitan areas were met with micro and macro aggressions, safeguarding Black and White segregation in America's cities.

Social programs have become Jim Crow-era tools to protect Whites from the prospects of Black social mobility and desegregation. The Job Insurance Program, for example, offered financial assistance for individuals while employed, but could not be used by agricultural or domestic service workers, overwhelming Black professions. The loan programs offered by the FHA and VA provided the working and middle classes with low-cost mortgages, business loans and cash payments for living expenses, but disproportionally benefited White Americans.

Home loans, in particular, carried restrictions that prevented the insuring of suburban mortgages to Blacks in the suburbs, as well as selling homes purchased through government assistance programs to Blacks. Even public housing was segregated by race to prevent integration. The explicitly racist governmental social welfare practices placed millions of dollars solely into the hands of White citizens, setting the boundaries of American cities and suburbs.

Jim Crow's control of social welfare programs, left Black Americans in a disadvantaged position socially, politically and economically. Further complicating matters is the irony that Black Americans were required to pay higher tax rates for social welfare programs too which they were denied access. The combination of being denied access to the social benefits of the New Deal, while simultaneously funding these programs for Whites proved detrimental to Black American's social mobility and economic development.

RED, BLACK, AND WHITE

The administration of the New Deal safeguarded segregation, by financially incentivizing White Americans to flee the Black urban migration and relocate to prime city real estate or the suburbs. As millions of Blacks fled the South to cities such as St. Louis, Chicago, Philadelphia, Detroit, and New York, they were met by racialized discrimination socially engineered by Jim Crow. To restrict the residential mobility of Blacks in cities and suburbs tactics such as redlining funnelled Black citizens into overpopulated urban enclaves, creating the *ghettos* and *barrios* present today. The discriminatory practices of redlining prevented Blacks from obtaining homes loans in certain residential areas based on the racial or ethnic composition of those areas.

The origins of redlining, the biased pattern of disinvestment and restrictive lending practices date back to the New Deal era and federal agencies such as the Federal Housing Authority (FHA). Roosevelt's racist redlining extended far beyond the FHA, to the entire mortgage industry. Bankers and realtors utilized redlining – literally shading Black areas red on maps and White areas blue – denying potential Black homeowners access to White neighbourhoods. White Americans were afforded middle-class opportunities to own homes subsidized by White and Black taxes dollars, while African-Americans fought for both access and rights. Denying Black citizens access to federal and private loan programs restricted home ownership to certain urban areas.

The Jim Crow Effect manipulated public policies, government programs, and democratic standards to maintain racial segregation. The racial composition of today's neighbourhoods, urban and suburban, directly result from the Jim Crow Effect. The social category of the Negro constructed during slavery and slightly upgraded under Reconstruction, could never be described as free. Battles for Blacks to exercise their civil rights, directly shaped cities, but also predetermined access to quality schools and economic opportunities. The racial composition of our cities, socially engineered by the Jim Crow Effect, prove to be a permanent marker on the moral compass of democracy.

JUSTIN A. COLES

2. THE COSTS OF WHISTLING, ORANGE JUICE, AND SKITTLES

An Anti-Black Examination of the Extrajudicial Killings of Black Youth

African Americans have always been distrustful of law enforcement officers and institutions. As a result of post-racial narratives, particularly those advanced during the Obama presidency, many people believe that African American concerns regarding police brutality are illegitimate and that everyone is viewed equally in the eye of the law. As with other systems rooted in racial tension in America (e.g. educational equity, gentrification, access to healthcare) the systemic policing of Black bodies and communities is frequently shrouded in ahistoricism.

A lack of concern or disregard for, or even lack of knowledge of, historical events, which in many cases have lasting structural effects on society. In this chapter, I reject ahistorical perspectives that position police brutality as isolated and rare incidents and argue that the anti-black history of America is present in every interaction between a Black person and law enforcement. When seeking to understand why African Americans distrust and resent the criminal justice system (police, courts, and prisons), we must consider the history of Blacks and policing in this country.

HISTORICIZING ANTI-BLACKNESS AND POLICING

Birthed in the image of white supremacy, America is both a settler colonial and anti-Black nation. The presence of Native Americans obstructed European settlers' access to land, which led to mass genocide. Later, enslaved Blacks augmented the wealth of white Colonial slave owners, who lacked of knowledge of the land and exploited Black people for free labour. So, the foundation of the U.S. and how privilege and disadvantage is bestowed upon groups is built on land theft and Native American removal as well as the social construction of Blacks as necessary, yet disposable beings, a construction that continues today.

The socially constructed notion of Blacks as less than human – therefore rendering them disposable – dictated the ways in which Black bodies were controlled and policed during chattel slavery. Slave-owners and any white individuals on or beyond plantations had full dominance over the body of the slave. Literature clearly documents the existence of Slave Patrols, which were created to ensure that law and order was maintained.

© KONINKLIJKE BRILL NV, LEIDEN, 2018 | DOI 10.1163/9789004378735_002

In addition to restricting the literal movement of Black bodies, Slave Patrols worked to concretize the notion that Blacks were property, not just of slave owners, but property of whiteness, the nation. The humanity of the slave was disregarded and any attempt of the Black population at this time to subvert this power dynamic was violently obstructed. The desire for Black people to be free, which would disrupt the capitalist gains of the American economy, birthed the need for relentless policing of the population.

Through branding an entire population as needing to be policed, the image of the uncivilized, unruly Black person came to define American ideals of criminality. Even after slavery was abolished, African Americans were propelled into a society where they were legally free, yet still subjected to tactics of control and surveillance. This revealed itself through measures such as Black Codes, Jim Crow Laws, and presently to what Michelle Alexander has coined *The New Jim Crow*.

The history of America is the history of control over the Black body: this nation is rooted in the policing of Black bodies. This tradition of policing has led officers and vigilante citizens to police Black people in ways that are brutal, irrational, and commonplace. Thus, African Americans understand the criminal justice system as the abusive, inhumane control of Black bodies that is the source of their distrust of law enforcement.

POLICE VIGILANTE BRUTALITY

Police brutality against Black bodies is a structural component of American life. It is well within the realms of the Black social imagination that in any encounter with law enforcement, at any moment, the Black body can be subjected to attack under the guise of law and order. When seeking to understand the distrust the Black community has towards law enforcement, we cannot see incidents of police brutality as separate acts, but again rather as a systemic structure that exists because the nation both allows and needs it. Indeed, seemingly countless cases in the U.S. reveal that police are seldom punished for these assaults, even when they end in death.

While police brutality as an extension of slave patrols is alarming, what concerns me most in addition to police brutality is vigilante brutality. In other words, I am concerned with how police brutality – as a result of anti-blackness – extends beyond police, giving everyday citizens the authority to be brutal towards Black people. Particularly after slavery, in the age of Reconstruction, vigilante groups such as the Ku Klux Klan (the Klan or KKK) who staunchly resisted racial equality, terrorized the Black community by means such as bombings and lynchings.

Groups and individuals like the Klan took it upon themselves to dispose of Black bodies, which in most cases had been either justified or completely overlooked by the criminal justice system. The Black body has been positioned as something unworthy of humanity – rooted in constructions of fear of the Black body based off the imagined danger it possesses. When it a vigilante kills a Black person, it is generally considered justified due to the anti-Black founding of the country that supports and created this context, an atmosphere centred on the collective disdain for Black people.

Anti-Blackness in America allows any act of Black death – no matter who is responsible – to be excusable. This justifying phenomenon is at the root of the mistrust between Black communities and the U.S. criminal justice system. To better explain vigilante brutality and its connection to African Americans' distrust of law enforcement, I highlight the extrajudicial killings of Emmett Till, Latasha Harlins, and Trayvon Martin.

THE EXTRAJUDICIAL KILLINGS OF EMMETT, LATASHA, AND TRAYVON

The double-sided American coin of white supremacy and anti-Blackness has created the path for vigilantes to kill Black children since the founding of America. I use the cases of Emmett, Latasha, and Trayvon because they have each occurred in three distinct time periods of U.S. history. These stories provide a basis to reject false ideals of 21st century racial progress, where African Americans have a new-found reason to trust the criminal justice system. How can a Black parent, family, or community, trust and support law enforcement officers when this system systemically participates in and justifies the death of Black children?

In 1955, two white men, 24-year-old Roy Bryant and 36-year-old John William Milam, in Money, Mississippi took 14-year-old Emmett Till from the house of his great uncle. Varying accounts allege that Emmett whistled at Bryant's wife and/or uttered a phrase such as *bye Baby*. The men took Emmett to a barn where they beat him, shot him, and then threw him in the Tallahatchie River with a seventy-pound fan from a cotton gin tied around his neck.

In 1991, 15-year-old Latasha Harlins was murdered by Soon Ja Du, a 51-year-old female Korean storeowner in Los Angeles, California. Ja Du suspected that Latasha was stealing orange juice, but store surveillance footage and eyewitness accounts revealed that Harlins had money for the juice in her hand. Ja Du assaulted Latasha by grabbing her backpack and throwing a stool. After the scuffle, Latasha placed the juice on the counter and proceeded to exit the store. As Latasha was walking out, Ja Du shot her in the back of the head.

In 2012, 17-year-old Trayvon Martin was shot by George Zimmerman, a 28-year-old Hispanic white male. Trayvon was returning to the house of his father's fiancée while carrying Skittles and a fruit drink. Zimmerman, program coordinator for the town's neighbourhood watch, called police to report that Trayvon was walking around looking suspicious and even suggested that he might be on drugs. Police told Zimmerman that he should not follow Trayvon. Moments later, the two got in a scuffle – as a result of Zimmerman continuing to follow him – which ended with Trayvon being shot in the chest at close range.

7

MURDERED BLACK CHILDREN, FREE VIGILANTES

The murderers of Emmett believed that a Black boy must be taught a deadly lesson – one that would leave him unrecognizable – for daring to flirt with a white woman. The murderer of Latasha believed a Black girl with a backpack must have been planning to steal, which deserved a bullet to the brain. The murderer of Trayvon could not conceptualize a Black boy who was not criminal, which prompted him essentially to hunt and kill the teen.

The lack of consequences for these children's murderers reveals the anti-Blackness at the root of this mistrust. Trayvon's murderer was found not guilty of second-degree murder. The men who killed Emmett, for example, were put on trial with an all-white, all-male jury and were acquitted. Shortly after the trial the men sold the story of how they did in fact kill Emmett. A jury sentenced Latasha's murderer to 16 years in prison for voluntary manslaughter. Judge Joyce Karlin rejected the jury's sentence, however, giving the murderer five years of probation, 400 hours of community service and a fine of $500.

The jury in this last case concluded that she was guilty, but the criminal justice system, via Judge Karlin, literally made the executive decision that Ja Du did not need to suffer. What Judge Karlin did not consider is the fact that Latasha and her family already experienced incomparable suffering the moment Ja Du's bullet entered Latasha's head. Was Latasha's death not enough to warrant her murderer's suffering? Structurally, Black lives do not matter to the criminal justice system and until they do, the Black community will continue to be suspicious of anything associated with law and order.

CONCLUSION

The U.S. criminal justice system is relentlessly anti-Black, which results in the inability of the African American community to conceptualize an existence where they would benefit from trusting law enforcement. In an anti-Black society, what transpired before the death of a Black child seldom matters in meting out justice. In matters of Black death, in the legacy of chattel slavery and policing Black bodies, it is already assumed that the life and liberties of the assailant were threatened in the interaction and more so, that the freedom of the assailant is more important to consider than the justice sought for the dead Black child. Justice for African Americans coming second to the justice of others contributes to Black suffering. Black suffering is then embedded within the criminal justice system; the suffering of non-Blacks is never allowed to happen in relation to Blacks.

EBONY ROSE

3. THE MYTH OF POST-EMANCIPATION

*Utilizing the 1857 Dred Scott Decision and the 2017 Chicago
Department of Justice Report to Examine Hyper-Policing,
Black Freedom, and Strategies for Resistance*

In 1857, the United States Supreme Court issued a landmark decision on Dred Scott v. Sandford, also known as the Dred Scott case. They concluded that Scott, as a slave taken by his master into the free part of the Louisiana territory, could not exercise the prerogative of a free citizen to sue in federal court. Chief Justice Robert B. Taney, was unsatisfied with the decision of only denying citizenship rights to slaves.

As a result, Taney took it one step further by arguing that *negroes*, are excluded, under the word *citizens* in the constitution. A negro, whose ancestors were imported into this country and sold as slaves, would never become a member of the political community. Resultantly he argued that they should not be recognized by the Constitution of the United States.

Chief Justice Taney considered enslaved Africans to be a subordinate and inferior class of beings, who had been subjugated by the dominant race (whites'), and were therefore justly and lawfully reduced to slavery for their benefit. One of Chief Justice Taney's conclusions in the Dred Scott decision of 1857, was that the negro has no rights that the white man is bound to respect. The Dred Scott decision more so than the Constitution, fixed race and ancestry (Black and African) to status (slave) and to personhood.

Taney supported the common idea that people from the continent of Africa were initially pre-ordinated by God and Christianity as inferior, and their only purpose was to be used as property. And later secular justification for this coincided with the rise of the natural and social sciences as the natural order of things and later biology and economics will pay a role in creating representations reinforced in law of the inherent inferiority of African originated peoples.

Consequently, for Taney, people of the United States and citizens were synonymous and excluded both slaves and freed Black people. From the Dred Scott decision on, Black people were permanently captured in the non-human/non-citizen/slave position. Too little consideration has been given to linking race, law, slavery and the dehumanization of African Americans communities within law enforcement agencies. One consequence is stale debates over community policing and police reform instead of police abolition, and Black emancipation.

© KONINKLIJKE BRILL NV, LEIDEN, 2018 | DOI 10.1163/9789004378735_003

This chapter challenges the dominant and pervasive commonsense that the Civil War ended the slave-like treatment of Black people in the United States of America. In addition, I argue that no post-emancipation society exists where Black people have rights, and freedoms guaranteed by the constitution. Moreover, the concept of Black dehumanization helps explain the lack of Black citizenship in the United States.

With this framework, I evaluate the techniques police engage in when dealing with the Black community; I argue that the engagement is oppositional to Black humanity. Black people, especially those living in economically isolated and high poverty concentrated communities concretely experience the symptoms of anti-Black racism in the form of hyper-policing, resulting in the premature death of their kin.

In 2017, Black people still occupy this questionable non-human/non-citizen/ slave category which allows the police to suspend their obligation to the law when policing Black communities. Using Black people's experiences with police in the 2017 Investigation of the Chicago Police Department, Department of Justice report, I will prove how and why Black people experience the police in *the afterlife of slavery*. In *the afterlife of slavery* an ex-slave society like the U.S. still possess slave-like socio-political and economic characteristics in the 21st century.

Black communities experience the police as an occupying force, that exemplifies the myth of post-emancipation society. The police function as 21st century slave catchers. Consequently, Black communities have used alternative methods rather than the courts and the law (e.g., Restorative and Transformative justice social justice methods) that prioritize restoration, healing, accountability, justice, atonement, and transformation.

U.S. police violate the Constitutional rights of Black people with impunity, operating under this historical commonsense that Black people in the United States are excused from citizenship. The 2017 Chicago Department of Justice report concluded that the Chicago Police Department, for example, engages in a pattern or practice of force in violation of the Constitution. Among the most egregious uses of deadly force the Department of Justice reviewed were incidents in which CPD officers shot at suspects who presented no immediate threat. Despite these findings, the police see no violation of constitutional rights of Black people.

Upon, further inspection, one discovers that the Black community, who are descendent from Africa, who came to this country as slaves, have to question why their communities are subject to excessive state violence by the police with no regard for their lives. The police, as historically evolved from the slave patrol will never protect and serve Black people and their communities. The police were not created for that function. During the days of slavery, the views of Supreme Court Chief Justice Taney were common.

Now compare this to how police treat Black people today. The *2017 Chicago Department of Justice report* recorded residents sharing their experiences with the DOJ. The DOJ has on record Black people telling them that they perceive the police as dog catchers. This means the police treat members of the Black community like dogs. In another example, Black residents reported treatment so demeaning they felt dehumanized. One Black resident told the investigators that when it comes to CPD, there is no respect of our humanity as Black people.

The Chicago Police Department, U.S. DOJ reports that Chicago does not investigate the residents of Chicago complaints against the CPD. Moreover, the CPD lacks a systemic accountability system to the point that many officers will never receive a warning for their recklessness. The question is why should the CPD investigate cases of people who the police routinely calls "n*****," "animal," or "pieces of (expletive)." A mindset like this has desensitized many officers, detaching them from the humanity of the Black people they serve, setting the stage for the use of excessive force.

The editors of this book ask the question "Whose lives really matter, and how do we move forward?" For those of us who make it our responsibility and intellectual mission to contemplate bigger philosophical issues related to these questions, we must understand how Black lives do not matter. More importantly, we must come to the realization that Black lives never mattered. The society at large, historically and currently, continue not to recognize Black people and their children as a part of the nation of citizens. The most egregious uses of deadly force by CPD will not change if Black people are not recognized and treated as humans.

The report demonstrates that the CPD's pattern of practice of unreasonable force and systemic deficiencies falls heaviest on the Black and Latino neighborhoods on the South and West Sides of Chicago. People in Chicago's downtown areas only rarely see this type of policing. Everyone in Chicago know this. This is a common experience of most Black communities in this country.

In the Department of Justice investigation of CPD, several recommendations were made to the city to improve policing. In short, all the recommendations involved a reversal of current practices. In theory this sounds nice, but nothing will change for the Black citizens in the city of Chicago. What then can these citizens of Chicago do to reaffirm their lives and their humanity in a system which denies them this every day? There are already movements in Chicago to implement other strategies for handling behaviors and practices that violate the community norms established through Restorative and Transformative justice.

Restorative justice is a process that focuses on rehabilitation of offenders through reconciliation with victims and the community at large. The most well-known technique for rehabilitation and reconciliation is the use of Peace Circles. Since crime hurts, it should also have a chance to heal. Restorative justice is concerned with assigning to the offender active responsibility. This means that rather than being told they committed a crime and then being punished for their indiscretion, offenders are asked to acknowledge their crime and try to atone for it.

The Peace Circle is a Restorative justice model that like other practices is used to discuss conflict holistically and solve problems. Peace circles emphasize healing and learning through collective group practices. The goal is to identify the root problems of harmful behaviors and restore the community to a place of calm, not relying on the police, since often the criminal justice system turns first to punishment

11

and retribution. Moreover, Transformative Justice takes a bolder approach, instead of simply seeking to restore things to the pre- crime environment, transformative justice seeks to transform society for the better.

It seeks to change the larger social structures as well as the personal structures of those involved. A systemic commitment for Restorative and Transformative Justice can force the United States to reckon with its unjustness and anti-Black racism of our current criminal justice system. By doing this, this nation will recognize that if there is racism in this society there is no justice whatsoever. The transformative approach not only offers healing and active responsibility to the perpetrator, the victim, and the community, but it also begins to take power away from the police and into the hands of the citizens to practice accountability and responsibility.

What would happen if those in Black communities dreamt of a society more grand and spectacular, innovative and imaginative than the one we currently live in? What would it take for the 40 million Black people in this country to begin in the belly of the beast, laying the foundation for an autonomous community controlled by its residents. They will only be accountable and responsible to each other.

Ideally, this community will be self-sufficient, and in the far future, sovereign from the United States. Restorative and Transformative Justice practices are now used as alternatives to the legal punitive practices in the status quo. In the long run, another path can be charted; brick-by-brick, stone-by-stone Black people build a world without police in their communities. Without police, Black people will no longer represent the symbolic and economic designation as the non-human others in a slave society.

I know this is a radical proposition, but we need radicalism now more than ever. Police abolition is the first step to making Black Lives Matter. For actual freedom, police abolition must be put on the table. Without the police, Black people's social imaginations will run wild, to create a free society. Only then can we discover who we really are as a people and a nation of humans, and therefore citizens.

ROLANDA L. WARD AND ISIAH MARSHALL JR

4. EAST VS. WEST

The Industrious and Inconsistent Rising of Buffalo, New York

The contemporary spatial, economic, and social segregation of Buffalo, New York, can certainly be attributed to the typical sociological and urban planning causes: decreased economic conditions, high poverty, and increasing educational achievement gaps. Like many urban centers, the struggles of New York's second largest city are steeped in failing social and economic policies, as well as shifts in employment opportunities for those outside of the networks of higher education. Some might argue that these factors result in higher representation of people of color in our criminal justice system, as well as within the social service system.

These common explanations allow discourse pertaining to causes and solutions, but rarely address the historical and contemporary failures of government entities who promote status quo governing and stagnated initiatives. As time moves and neighborhoods remain the same, it is imperative to recall the history of the city and question the impact of community leaders' decisions as naive, haphazard, or even deliberate. This chapter explores the history of Buffalo's economy on the black community and how political abandonment as well as human and social capital disinvestment are to blame for the social conditions strangling black people.

Buffalo's early history is a rich one, serving as an entry point to early transportation waterways. Buffalo became the place to live in America, and within a short period of time, the city became home to many millionaires building lavish homes along Delaware Avenue, Millionaires Row, some of which remain today. Even as Buffalo swelled, the city became home to several large ethnic groups. Polish, Germans, Italians, and Irish settled into various neighborhoods and cultivated cultural traditions that still shape the customs and rituals of the city over one hundred years later.

The early ethnic diversification of the city created distinct neighborhoods that were difficult to penetrate or created ripe situations for white flight. As southern blacks shifted from agrarian to industrialized sources of income, many blacks found a new home in Buffalo. Like other east coast cities, Buffalo was home to many manufacturing jobs. The labor markets provided those in the great migration economic opportunities that were not available in the south, and as a result, many blacks prospered and built middle-class lifestyles in neighborhoods that were separate from earlier ethnic groups. As the city grew, so did spatial separation.

© KONINKLIJKE BRILL NV, LEIDEN, 2018 | DOI 10.1163/9789004378735_004

The impact of spatial separation on Buffalo would be tested as the economic boom started to decline. As the need for steel was no longer great, Buffalo soon became a rustbelt city, where companies abandoned ship and left skeletons of empty factories and devastated families resulting in a decline in population. This shift in the economic foundation of the region pushed people with means to southern states to find other employment opportunities; those who remained sought assistance through the welfare system and or secured low-wage earning jobs.

The impact of this decline would befall rapidly upon the black community and would serve as the early nail in its coffin. These outcomes would transform the community's ability to be self-sufficient and even robust. Black males who shifted from southern cotton picking to manufacturing jobs were left without a safety net as their acquisition of those earlier manufacturing jobs was never really based upon education completion, but a willingness to work long and hard in blue collar jobs.

As more and more blacks were laid-off from jobs that netted them homes, cars, and stable communities, those same status symbols became burdensome. The impact was felt even more so among younger black males; they would never have an opportunity to work manufacturing jobs that would net them economic self-sufficiency like their elder family members. In addition, replacement positions were not on the forefront and were certainly not being discussed.

The deterioration of Buffalo's economic security, coupled with the drug attack on urban centers across America, meant Buffalo's black communities were now under siege. Soon the symptomatology of poverty would become visible and the disease of poverty would become prevalent. The city soon started to transform and the indicators of poverty became Buffalo's phenotype, with the black community now disproportionality represented in the courts, not because of a change in the communities' values and norms, but rather because of failed political representation.

When employment opportunities trickle to a stop or trickle to other communities, it is no surprise that poverty becomes infectious. Crime, housing, education, and family compositions transformed right before the community's eyes. The large, two family structures that distinctly defined Buffalo were abandoned by homeowners, mainly white, who moved to emerging suburbs.

As vacancy rates increased in the city, the facades of houses became weathered. Soon these homes became sitting tinder boxes and were thought to be more valuable on fire. Overtime the geography and demography of the black community looked unrecognizable: fewer black men, more vacant lots, overgrown grass, and boarded up houses, while other, mainly white, communities successfully weathered Buffalo's economic retreat.

As black families attempted to move about the city in search of safe and secure housing, white flight also ensued. Soon urban blight sprawl assumed what is known as the East Side and an infamous reputation would thereafter isolate the black community even further. Even though the East Side is not simply one neighborhood, it would intentionally be labeled as one community: the black neighborhood. And to those living outside of the East Side, it would become the neighborhood you don't want to live in, drive through, work in, or send your kids to school in, that is, if you had a choice.

A NEWCOMER'S EXPERIENCE

Many opinionated bloggers describe Buffalo, NY as a city that continues to have major problems with race, opportunity, tourism, diversity and the list goes on and on. In fact, when in conversation about visiting Buffalo, some colleagues have mentioned that they cannot get any feeling for the place. With all that being said, Buffalo is now a place of challenge and growth; moreover, it has been ranked as one of most inexpensive cities in the country and a new chic haven for millennials.

Settling in Buffalo one has a choice of older, well maintained apartments or very inexpensive real estate. One intact African-American neighborhood on Buffalo's East side, Hamlin Park, is well publicized in magazines and local papers. Hamlin Park, like many other neighborhoods in cities, started as predominantly white in the late 1800s. The neighborhood is surrounded by Canisius College, a few scattered businesses, and several churches.

The 1950s and 60s brought change in the racial dynamics of Hamlin Park. Many white families moved to the suburbs while Hamlin Park transformed itself into the Mecca for the black elite of Buffalo. Like many inner-city neighborhoods, however, Hamlin Park also experienced blight and instability issues during the late 1970's through the 1990s. Having lived in other areas of the country where the real estate was quite expensive, Buffalo's low cost of living became a major draw. Main Street literally divides Buffalo. On the west side of Main Street the rents range from $900–$2000 and the rents on the east side of Main Street range from $350–$750.

It seemed like overnight the development in the city started to happen. The city's waterfront came under development; the medical campus expanded and became a corridor; and for the first time, several non-black families were observed moving into Hamlin Park, a national historic community. Many single, white men with money moved into several vacant spaces and wealthy parents purchased homes for their college aged children. Many of the new inhabitants were now being labeled as "Urban Pioneers."

Several news stories featured young white couples who had moved into the community to take advantage of the city's one dollar home buying incentive program. Since Hamlin Park is relatively close to downtown and the medical corridor, it soon started to be a place where construction projects and new residents indicated a changing community. Although the press was positive for the Hamlin Park community, many of the life-long residents felt that their community was only highlighted because white people were now moving in, feeling they had been maintaining their properties for years, and no one came to do a story about their success.

In 2016, as new professional opportunities emerged, keeping the house in Buffalo, NY was a no brainer; the community feeling in Hamlin Park was the driving force. At the same time, news stories about gentrification and parking issues around the medical corridor, rising rental costs, demolition of old buildings, construction cranes, former residents coming back to live, opening of new retail spaces, and several other things that "signified" a change for the region became ever more visible.

These observations seemed familiar. Buffalo's changes are similar to the changes observed in Washington, DC in the late 1990s early 2000s. DC's renaissance caused many people of color to be displaced and relocated from communities of origin; it caused those who were on the margins of society to be overlooked even more. Many lost their homes in city tax sales and the taxes increased so much that many of the homeowners had to leave their communities.

African Americans during the elite days now see Hamlin Park as a sign of upward mobility. Many see it as a great place to settle when they land their first new job. They can network and remain in the center of town. However, one must think of the people in Hamlin Park who are not in the upwardly mobile category or those who are aging rapidly. As older African American people die out and their children sell the family home, oftentimes to the first investor or some young, white, wealthy person who wants to be close to work and close to the bars downtown, the neighborhood will change even more.

Though Hamlin Park is going through this transformation, seemingly for the better, the values of the community may soon be lost and it will become a not so welcoming place for those who originally called it home. In the final analysis, this can be viewed as a continuation of black people being forced into situations in which they have no choice about and in situations where their elected officials rarely sought out economic policies that would invest in the preservation of the black community.

THE ANALYSIS

The exploration of Buffalo's inconsistent rising brings moments of pure exasperation. Analysis of its inconsistencies provides insights about who is to blame. Not immune to the politics of other large cities across America, Buffalo shares similar explanations: leadership, economic disinvestment, and a discontinuity of protective social capital.

Are there enough protective social factors among Buffalo's black community? One protective factor that needs exploring is the social capital of the black middle class. The question is not about where was the Black middle class, but was the black middle class large and strong enough to block gentrification? The answer is no. Buffalo has always been a working-class community.

Its history of manufacturing isolated, both physically and socially, individuals living on the East side, resulting in deep and severe systemic barriers that kept residents from modernization opportunities that required retraining and/or the acquisition of higher education. Furthermore, when you layer on Buffalo's traditional labor market, significant inclines in poverty, significant declines in high school graduation rates, and rising early feminization of families, the black middle class, by itself, can never promote the bridges to networks and resources that might slow or even stunt the reclassification of traditional black neighborhoods.

16

Blaming the victim, the black community, for the dismantalization of its own communities is not the answer. Instead, questions about Buffalo's leadership and their governing through intentional geographic economic renaissance policies must be more deeply analyzed. The economic boom that is taking place in Buffalo is happening in communities of color that are now whitening. Cheap land with low taxes is now prime real estate. Economic investment instead of social investment is the preferred.

Resale of houses to outsiders is preferred instead of the last resort. These practices are strangling traditional communities and, furthermore, magnifying the spatial and economic segregation of the black community. These policies and practices produce two Buffalos: one for economically prosperous (white) and one for the economically forgotten (black).

Although some may argue that the calamities and injustices that befall people in the city of Buffalo are self-inflicted, one cannot negate the power of structural inequalities and the impact of masked racism that have existed in these communities. We argue that policies and programs will do very little to correct these concerns if the dominant society does not identify its own internalized and oppressive view of the black community and work to create a new history that includes economic equity for the East side.

GEOFFREY L. WOOD

5. HISTORICAL CATEGORICAL INEQUALITY

The Creation of Two Segregated Cities within an Urban Centre

It has been argued that historical categorical inequality was created in American Cities, and exacerbated by several factors over time. Although segregation has been illegal in most places in the U.S. for the past fifty years, cities in America remain divided among demographic factors, which continue to divide and paralyse the nation even today.

This essay discusses the ways in which historical categorical inequality has taken root in American Cities leading to higher levels of segregation over time. Then, the discussion shifts to recent changes in American ideology and dialogue, which continue to strengthen the death grip of segregated cities on urban residents in America. Finally, the essay concludes with recommendations on potential solutions to deal with the pressing problems in American Cities.

Historical categorical inequality established itself in cities centuries ago. Early American Cities were often segregated into white and black communities. Blacks and whites were not permitted to live in the same areas in many cities due to de jure segregation laws. In the 1890s, the U.S. Supreme Court ruled that blacks and whites could live in separate neighbourhoods, go to separate schools, and due to this have different levels of neighbourhood opportunities, as long as these separations were equal.

This ruling was also consistent with the beliefs and values of most people at the time. There were no mechanisms, however, which allowed for the development of separate, but equal places. Well-established categorical inequality with dominant and subordinate groups historically in place prevented any sort of equality from taking root. In fact, this segregation of American Cities by law allowed for the development of schools, neighbourhoods, and enclaves within cities, which were indeed separate, but never equal.

Absent the Supreme Court's involvement, however, neighbourhood and residential patterns of segregation by race were long since established by ideology, law, and tradition. These ideologies, laws, and traditions kept in place a pattern of neighbourhood and residential segregation, which carried over into every aspect of urban life. Although the U.S. Supreme Court reversed itself in the 1950s, precedent and damage from dividing people by race and to a lesser extent by social class had been well fortified, and continues to this day.

© KONINKLIJKE BRILL NV, LEIDEN, 2018 | DOI 10.1163/9789004378735_005

From the beginning in these cities, a dominant and subordinate group of people divided by race was established, and then codified into societal, organizational, and personal interactions. Historical categorical inequality was established the moment these dominant and subordinate groups were set, as this divide became the determining factor of social life. Categorical inequality became institutionalized in the American City.

Individuals were not required to harbor prejudice beliefs or act on discrimination, as an unequal institutionalized system of dominant and subordinate groups thrived. Blacks and whites lived in separate neighbourhoods, went to separate schools, had different groups and opportunities for socializing, and even developed distinct ideologies and cultures. Importantly, these schools and neighbourhoods by race in cities were never initially equal, and as time passed, became more unequal as income, wealth, power, and access to resources pooled in dominant group communities.

Although de jure segregation has become less prominent, American Cites of various sizes remain divided by race. Throughout the years, the laws of segregation by race and the era of Jim Crow laws have begun to fade. The categorical inequality established and perpetuated over time remained. School districts and neighbourhoods remain stratified along dimensions of race and class. Given that school districts rely on local property taxes from neighbourhoods for up to fifty percent of their funding, disparities of income and wealth within neighbourhoods create schools with significant levels of differences in resources.

Whiter, wealthier neighbourhoods with high property values contribute much greater resources to their schools, than do their Blacker, poorer counterparts. Adding to this problem is that the other fifty percent of school funding comes from federal and state sources. While these sources contribute funds mostly equally to schools, the real resource differential among schools is at the local level.

These differences in resource levels explain some of the quality differences between neighbourhood schools. Differences in school funding within cities by neighbourhood contributes not just to school quality, but perpetuates differences in dominant and subordinate access to resources at interpersonal, organizational, and societal levels. It is well established, for example, that one of the best predictors of academic success is the zip code in which one lives.

In American Cities, we have created two school tracks based on historical categorical inequality. In addition to historical categorical inequality, de facto segregation by race and class, and neighbourhood disparities in school wealth and quality, there have been salient changes in ideology, political sentiment, and attitudes toward subordinate groups.

Throughout the latter half of 2016, attitudes toward women, minorities, immigrants, and gay people have coalesced to perpetuate deeper categorical inequality in urban centres. While some of this is attributable to a dangerous and ridiculous rhetoric from political leadership during a deeply contested election cycle, important factors divide people living in American Cities, allowing for even higher levels of segregation.

From an ideological standpoint, one of the most important of these is the rise of white nationalism, or the alt-right movement. Throughout the 2016 election cycle, Donald Trump demonized Mexican immigrants, women, and Muslims appealing to deep seeded feelings of xenophobia, racism, sexism, and religious superiority. Some of this may be in reaction to the Obama-era, as racist tensions between dominant and subordinate groups simmered below the surface. Interestingly the rhetoric was focused on distinctions between Blacks and whites as class-based rhetoric did not resonate with whites as well as established established racist sentiments.

From a political standpoint, there are examples of segregation rhetoric and policy suggestions from the Trump Administration. One of these is the executive order blocking immigration to the U.S. from predominantly Muslim counties. Reactions to this executive order included protests and court action blocking the order from taking effect. The Trump Administration orchestrated a second iteration of the ban, with partial success. While Trump argued vehemently that first two bans were not Muslim Bans, statements to the contrary made during the campaign and later in court documents, as well as the political discourse and rhetoric from alt-right and conservative talk radio show hosts demonstrates otherwise.

Another example is the insistence of President Trump on building a wall between the U.S. and Mexico on the border to prevent immigration into the U.S., catering to anti-immigrant sentiments with this action, yet far more immigrant come to the U.S. by airplanes, than across the U.S.-Mexico border. Finally, recent rhetoric and hateful speech directed at women by President Trump has created extreme tension in American Cities as women react through protest toward these hateful actions.

Political leaders continue to divide Americans by race and gender as opposed to class. While one percent of the population receives 50% of the income and possesses 80% of the wealth, Americans continue to focus on divisions by race and gender, ignoring extreme levels of inequality which cut across race and gender categories. The tale of two Americas is represented well in the tale of divided cities, as residents fight for better neighbourhoods and schools, yet focus on outdated patterns of residential segregation, rather than working together across race, gender, neighbourhood, and school district lines for the betterment of the entire community.

Although there are extreme differences in power, income, wealth, and neighbourhood resources for Americans, much focus remains on segregating cities by race. Almost every major American City has neighbourhoods and schools segregated by race, seen every night on local news. We constantly hear the rhetoric of winners and losers based on divisions in American Cities, preventing unity across race, gender, and neighbourhood. As long as dominant and subordinate groups continue to socially reproduce the same system over time, we will continue to see the fracturing of bones in communities unable to heal from these historical wounds.

There may be potential solutions which could reduce the degree of racial residential segregation in order to reduce the reliance on previously established categories of inequality. One solution is the firm rejection by both dominant and subordinate groups of segregation by race. If urban residents recognized they had more in common with their neighbours who live in the same place, rather than differences by race alone, levels of unity in these places would likely increase.

While distinctions by race are socially constructed, differences by social class on levels of power, income, wealth, and neighbourhood privilege are far greater disparities in U.S. Society. Urban residents seem to be less class conscious than they are race conscious. The rise in vitriolic political rhetoric dividing Americans by race and gender, importantly, has worked quite well at keeping the focus away from real differences in power, income, and wealth.

U.S. media continues to focus on inner-city street crime and drugs at the local level. The flow of immigrants across the border at the state level, and the fear of terrorism from Muslim refugees at the national level. These distractions keep us from focusing on real differences in resources between dominant and subordinate groups, which have grown from the roots of categorical inequality over time.

Divisive political rhetoric and sexist language have also contributed to the continued segregation of American Cities. Insulting remarks about women and gay peoples continue to shape the vernacular of discourse in communities. These remarks were often stated by President Trump during the election campaign, and were aimed as galvanizing support of white, conservative men (and some women) who may have become disillusioned about their life chances, and are looking for someone to blame for their plight.

In January 2017, as a reaction, gay and women lead groups began to push back in ways not seen in a generation. These groups coalesced to make clear statements of resistance through protests across cities toward this harmful and destructive rhetoric of right-wing political groups. Nationwide protests have helped to illustrate that race, gender, and sexual orientation are not the real dividing factors of urban residents, but that issues of power, income, wealth should be the central focus of systemic change.

Historical categorical inequality has led to the creation and social reproduction of segregated cities. This has led to urban areas deeply divided by race, with separate schools and huge differentials in income, power, and wealth. Yet, reactions to dominant rhetoric and ideology may lead to changes. As urban residents react to the divisive ideologies of the political right, segregated city residents are able to become more aware of the importance of social class position in their daily lives.

As these residents realize the fight should not be over race, gender, and sexual orientation, but instead over income, power, and wealth, real systemic changes may be possible. Although conflicts over race and gender are related to those of class, class is the salient concept that maps best to conflicts in segregated cities. It is time for residents of American Cities to move beyond divisions of race and gender, and realize the importance of class in such conflicts.

MELINDA JACKSON-JEFFERSON AND DEONDRA WARNER

6. SEGREGATION THEN, SEGREGATION NOW

A Tale of Two Cities within One Urban Area

The crises of inequality facing our nation today in education, corrections, and the labor market are closely intertwined with our reemerging racial divisions. Since slavery, in our society, the black population has been portrayed as violent criminals, thugs, and hoodlums by the media, the community, and law officials. This portrayal is not unique to the southern region, but can be seen in various forms across the United States.

Black Americans only make up approximately 12 percent of the general population in the United States and more specifically, roughly 33 percent of the population in Louisiana but they account for more than half of all arrests for violent crimes, and almost half of all inmates in state and federal correctional facilities. In Louisiana, over 60 percent of all inmates in the local prisons are African Americans. This is one piece of evidence that shows that we are not living in a post-racial society.

Minority communities, particularly those where African-Americans reside, are often characterized by high crime rates, poor social services, and dilapidated housing. Furthermore, they are frequently viewed as the most dangerous and unsafe areas within the general public. If the city is not divided, then how do we conceptualize what is happening in our neighborhoods as it relates to the education, justice and housing?

SEGREGATED, UNEDUCATED, & INCARCERATED

Baton Rouge serves as a remarkable case study given that it represents some of most economically disadvantaged, uneducated, crime-infested, and segregated areas in the state. The city itself is a symbol of racial inequality, with unequal opportunities made available to black residents and racial disparities among social institutions. This high-crime southern city is ranked amongst the top ten most segregated areas in the United States.

For instance, approximately a third of African American residents are living in neighbourhoods comprised of 90 percent or more Blacks, and over 50 percent of the White population resides in neighbourhoods that are more than 90 percent White. The city is roughly 50/50 black/white, however, the public school systems are 80 percent black. White parents enrolled their kids in private and magnet schools at rates two times higher than Black parents, which contributes considerably to the overall patterns of segregation in many communities.

© KONINKLIJKE BRILL NV, LEIDEN, 2018 | DOI 10.1163/9789004378735_006

It is hard to determine whether or not the residents of the city intentionally sought ways to separate with regard to class and colour, but it is apparent that this division exists. The city is so racially segregated that affluent white residents proposed seceding to incorporate as a new town called St. George. While unsuccessful, the proposed town would have become and independent school district in the south-eastern area with more than 50% of students having been white and fewer than 25% would have been black. The median household income of a house in St. George city would have been $30,000 higher than that of black residents in surrounding communities.

The racial divide within the city of Baton Rouge is also evident with respect to the enormous amount of crime in neighbourhoods also marked with poverty, under resourced schools, and single-parent households. An increasing number of black residents live in poverty, roughly one in five. Of those living in poverty, more than half are single women with no husband present. Children from single parent households are more likely to drop out of school, become teenage parents themselves, and experience cognitive, emotional, and social problems.

Like the racial disparity seen in the educational system, the criminal justice system is another institution in which blacks are not afforded the same opportunities as their white counterparts. Blacks are almost three times more likely to be arrested than any other race in the local area. Additionally, black residents are linked to the majority of violent crimes in the city and they represent a disproportionate amount of all inmates in local and state prisons. This disparity is also true for nonviolent crimes.

In 2011, the District Attorney blocked a bill that would have reduced the amount of time spent in jail for people who committed non-violent offenses before approaching parole, a measure that could have saved the city millions of dollars. In the state of Louisiana, having three drug convictions could get an individual life without the possibility of parole, and three nonviolent criminal offenses could mean life in prison without early release. Louisiana has the highest incarceration rate in the country and sadly, this rate continues to rise.

An enormous number of black citizens are swept into the criminal justice system by local police officers conducting drug operations primarily in impoverished communities of colour. This system appears to have been designed to remove African Americans from the competitive labour force in society and as a result create more jobs for whites. The criminal justice system brands blacks as criminals and then it engages in all the practices that we supposedly left behind. Once an individual is labelled a felon, s/he is subjected to discrimination in terms of employment, housing, and education.

African American men are part of a growing under-caste who are locked up and locked out of mainstream society, which in turn has a devastating impact on African American communities. Residents living in extremely poor areas bear a double burden. Not only do they struggle with their own poverty, but also their surrounding communities have fewer job opportunities, lower-performing schools, higher crime rates, and more public health problems.

Living in a deprived neighbourhood makes it that much harder to escape poverty. Needless to say, being taught in a poorly performing public school means that many low-income residents often enter the job force lacking the basic tools needed to function in society. While African-Americans have made significant growth in the labour force since slavery, there are still major disparities. For instance, African American high school graduates are 70 percent more likely to experience job loss than their white counterparts. When they do find a job they are often in job sectors with limited benefits. The unemployment rate for African Americans is twice that of whites.

Local police officers are more likely to target lower income communities in which African-Americans reside. This behaviour continues to allow black men to be incarcerated and absent from any form of political and social justice. The recent killing of Alton Sterling serves as the prime example of African-American men who have been deemed thugs, and whose lives are therefore considered to be of lesser worth. Black residents are likely to experience neglect and rudeness at the hands of the police. Consequently, residents of colour tend to be more fearful and distrusting of those individuals sworn to protect and serve them.

MOVING FORWARD: UNDERSTANDING HOW THE SYSTEM WORKS

After centuries of slavery, black people still suffer from an incapacity to understand how systems of power work in our country. The lesson our oppressors have been trying to teach us for years is that change only occurs when those with power benefit most. Through prisons, lack of education, and other social services, the power of the dominant group is sustained. Instead of investing in education and underprivileged schools, politicians have chosen instead to fund incarceration.

We have to stop relying on the white supremacy to solve our problems. No law will ever change the way white oppressors feel about people of colour. In moving forward, it is critical to understand that the failing institutions that exist in communities of colour are functioning as they were always intended – giving privilege to some (whites) while oppressing others (blacks). Prisons were created to remove Blacks from society for the purpose of exploitation rather than rehabilitation.

Consequently, it is critical, as scholars that we continue to educate and teach our Black students and children about the nature of their social position. Additionally, how might we think strategically within a society where race does matters. Through teaching allows them to be mindful of the constant change and unceasing hostility that Blacks encounter in nearly every social institution.

DISCUSSION

African American communities in Baton Rouge are troubled by a host of problems. These problems range from racial profiling by local officers to a disproportionate number of Black families living in poverty. African Americans are more likely to be victims of a crime and reside in disadvantaged neighborhoods where violent crime is more common.

Despite the Civil Rights Movement, the War on Poverty, and other episodic victories in the legislature, African Americans are still subject to institutionalized racism and discrimination, especially in the educational and criminal justice systems. Black residents lack access to the harvests of the richest nation on earth in today's allegedly just nation. At almost every juncture, the odds are stacked against them, resulting in too much unfilled potential and too many damaged lives.

PATRICIA MALONEY

7. THE DOUBLE PENALTY

How School and Neighborhood Segregation Affects Racial Conflict

Any student of American history can quickly identify *Brown v. The Board of Education of Topeka* (374 U.S. 483) as the 1954 Supreme Court case that overturned the separate but equal doctrine enshrined in *Plessy v. Ferguson* (1896), and made government-enforced school segregation illegal. Most have seen the pictures in social studies textbooks of some white people jeering at resolute black students as the black students entered schools. Modern Americans like to think of that time period as one of ignorance and racism. One might think, this could never happen today – isn't it wonderful the Supreme Court did away with segregation such a long time ago?

Except we have not progressed. Schools in America are, on average, actually more racially segregated today than they were in the mid-twentieth century, as much of the longitudinal demographic work of Douglas Massey and Andrew Beveridge makes clear. This is because the racial segregation ruled unconstitutional in *Brown* was considered *de jure* segregation, or segregation enforced by the rule of law, which was predominantly, although not solely, found in the southern United States.

Today's segregation is *de facto* segregation, or segregation that happens as a result and/or as a by-product of people's decisions. That is, this type of segregation is not governmentally enforced, which makes it much more insidious and difficult to combat. After *Brown*, education stakeholders attempted to integrate schools through myriad interventions: for example, busing, manipulating funding structures, and changing schools' catchment zones or the geographic regions surrounding schools from which students came, to maximize racial integration.

De facto segregation has many interwoven causes such as structural and interpersonal racism, housing costs, and federal redlining. There is another Supreme Court case, however, that is perhaps even more efficacious than *Brown* in affecting segregation in modern American schools: 1974's *Milliken v. Bradley* (418 U.S. 717). In this case, the Supreme Court held that school segregation can be allowed in the United States, provided that it is *de facto* and not *de jure*.

In other words, school districts cannot take affirmative actions to integrate schools like busing or re-drawing catchment zones to deliberately cause racial or class-based heterogeneity in schools. Thus, this case allowed schools to reflect the demographics of the geographic areas immediately around them, otherwise known as their catchment zones. So, it was not that the schools were segregated – it was that the neighborhoods were.

© KONINKLIJKE BRILL NV, LEIDEN, 2018 | DOI 10.1163/9789004378735_007

This social and judicial situation created the proverbial perfect storm. White flight was already well underway by 1974, yet was exacerbated by fear of the forced desegregation following *Brown* and then the sanction of neighborhood segregation created by *Milliken*. Indeed, there is research that indicates that, as school catchment zones were drawn and re-drawn with changing populations and town construction, school districts would gerrymander the zones, creating school segregation via deliberately chosen boundaries that created homogeneous neighborhoods in race and class.

THE EFFECTS OF WHITE FLIGHT AND DE FACTO SEGREGATION ON SCHOOLS

Public schools in the United States derive their funding from three main sources: federal funds, state funds, and local property taxes. Thus the value of the homes in the school's district or even its local catchment zone, implicitly affects the per pupil expenditure of a given school. While low-income schools can receive certain additional federal funds under laws like Title I of the *Elementary and Secondary Education Act of 1965*, they also may have to provide services to their students that higher-income schools do not, such as counseling or tutoring programs.

Students in low-income areas, who are predominantly students of color, consequently receive a double penalty. As any homeowner knows, the market value of a house is partially tied to the quality of the local school. Since the local school derives much of its funding from the local property taxes, which are based on the worth of the home, then the proverbial vicious cycle emerges. The houses in the predominantly white catchment zones become even more desired and expensive, while the homes in the predominantly minority catchment zones suffer a school penalty, causing them to lose worth at an even faster rate.

The effects of differential funding of education are not limited to monetary effects like housing. Low income schools often provide ameliorative resources to their students, while higher-income schools may be able to provide extra academic and extracurricular resources; this further widens the education gap between the races, since low-income schools disproportionately enroll students of color. In fact, growing evidence from the National Center for Education Statistics suggests that schools that predominantly enroll black students increase in both race and class homogeneity over time, compounding the disadvantages these students face.

Additionally, with fewer resources and more demands on educators' time, these students of color in low income schools are more likely to experience teacher churning. That is, they are likely to receive new teachers who may not yet have the proper experience to both teach a core curriculum to students who may be academically behind and simultaneously cope with the social needs of those students. Then, after gaining a few years of experience, these teachers leave for higher-income schools, more likely to enroll white students and perceived to be easier to teach in, ultimately leaving a vacuum for other new teachers to fill and creating the churning effect.

Until now this chapter has discussed how tracking and segregation occur within districts. Many districts, particularly rural and suburban districts, only have a few or even just one secondary school for all the high school age students in the district. This theoretically causes higher levels of heterogeneity based on race and class.

Indeed, this is the case – elementary schools in the United States are more segregated by race and class than secondary schools, predominantly because of elementary schools' smaller and more locally-based catchment zones that reflect neighborhood segregation. Thus, if we assume that heterogeneity of race and class in a school will fix many of the segregation-based issues mentioned above, this relative integration in secondary school should cause optimism.

This optimism should be short-lived. Most high schools in the United States have drawn upon academica tracking of students. Some of this tracking has at least the veneer of incorporating student and parent choice, such as allowing students to determine whether they wish to enroll in math classes beyond those mandated by the district.

Many of the more academic tracks (pre-AP, AP, or honors classes), however, draw upon classroom grades or scores on standardized test scores as well as teacher recommendations to serve as the means by which high school administrators determine the student's academic course load, which in turn has predictable effects for the student's later ability to attend college or have labor market success.

On its face, the above type of tracking seems functional and fair-minded. Theoretically, students should be placed in courses for which they have the proper mindset and preparation. Why put a student in an AP Calculus class if the student (a) has no interest and/or (b) had trouble in Algebra II?

This assumes, however, that all the students have equality of opportunity in terms of previous preparation, which is self-evidently not the case. This chapter has already discussed the phenomenon of teacher churning, which has obvious effects on students' learning and previous preparation, but there are other in-school factors that have decided impacts on students' ability to learn in school.

One of the other in-school factors is an increased focus on teaching to the test, or concentrating on subjects found in the yearly high stakes tests to the exclusion of other subjects which might cause greater excitement for learning among students. If the core subjects are not properly taught in the foundational years of elementary and middle school, then it is unsurprisingly that students perform worse in them during secondary school, particularly vexing in a labor market that is increasingly STEM-focused.

Beyond labor market success, a student who is well-grounded in civics and history is one who will be better able to advocate for herself as an adult. Of course, there are myriad other in-school and/or out-of-school factors that affect a student's ability to learn. Some of these factors include nutritional access, class size, discipline styles, and school culture. But, how do these differences in education translate into differences later in life?

SOCIAL AND LONG-LASTING EFFECTS BECAUSE OF *DE FACTO* SEGREGATION IN SCHOOLS

It seems obvious that decreased contact with other racial groups during formative early experiences should engender increased social distance and decreased trust. The often-cited contact hypothesis states that the more contact an individual has with members of another social group, particularly early in life, the less likely the individual will be to stereotype and fear members of that social group. If we apply that to schools in the United States, then our current *de facto* segregation can only increase conflicts between the races since individuals have learned to fear and distrust one another because of a lack of interaction during school years.

There is a dual mechanism at play. Early experiences cause increased social distance and proclivity for conflict between individuals in racial groups; they also cause a distrust of social structures in the disempowered group. Path dependency theory tells us that a person's initial interactions with a bureaucracy can solidify that person's attitudes towards all forms of bureaucracy associated with that power structure.

These areas might include city hall, medical personnel, or even law enforcement. Black students, or other students of color, many feel betrayed or "othered" by a social structure that was supposed to educate and prepare them for labor market success. The lack of an equal education and preparation for college/career likely causes anger and disengagement with all forms of civic and political life dominated by wealthy white people.

The effects of this lack of education and dual alienation from both the dominant racial group and social structures have multiple effects. Those without access to the legitimate labor market might turn to crime to fulfill financial needs, resulting in a criminal record and further distrust of law enforcement, which can then lead to a permanent removal from the legitimate labor market. A lack of trust in those in civic authority can lead to lowered voter participation rates, less access to preventative and emergency medical care, and distrust of their children's schools and education professionals.

Many see the recent increase in overt and covert racial conflict and the social conflict as shocking and unexpected. The seeds were sown decades prior, when the affirmative integration of schools was reversed in favor of allowing *de facto* neighborhood segregation to shape the racial homogeneity of modern American schools. *Brown* was a watershed decision in American law, but should not overshadow *Milliken*, which set the stage for the structural racism that allows such divisive racial and class homogeneity in schools. Such segregation and the enabled unequal education it creates only serves to increase racial conflict at large.

30

DEANNA HAYES-WILSON

8. ALL THAT GLITTERS ISN'T GOLD

It was the 1970s and any hint of segregation or separate but equal laws were officially dealt with by the passage of The Civil Rights Act. Any violation of separate but equal laws was immediately met by swift and brutal police actions. The old adage "Be careful what you ask for because you just might get it" comes to mind as the Civil Rights Act became a double-edged sword.

Instead of joining all fragmented ethnicities into one united nation, the act seemed to cause something unforeseen and unexpected in the Black community. The power base of community, a stronghold of Black strength since slavery, was destroyed. Although everyone has the legal right to live and attend schools anywhere, many urban cities are still segregated as white flight to suburban areas left Black citizens to contend with low performing, underfunded schools, blighted housing, and crime-infested inner-city lives.

The reality of a segregated city in the 1950s and 1960s forced Black people to live together and work together to secure the best possible education and life within the segregated walls. Ironically, there was little to no police presence in the segregated community or school but within these segregated walls, Black people had power. The community met in the gymnasium of the one Black school and made the important decisions affecting important voter issues.

I remember my father coming home late at night from his construction job 80 miles away and changing from his work clothes to a clean pair of slacks and pants. He and the other men in the community would meet in the gym with a list of the candidates running for office. The all-white candidates would vie for the opportunity to woo Black voters on Sundays in the pulpits of the major Black churches.

The discussion in the gym would go on, sometimes late into the night, but when the men left the gym, everyone had agreed on the candidate they would vote for in the upcoming election. The men would in turn go home and share the list with their wives and other members of the community who did not have representation at the meeting. When election time came, everyone voted at that same gymnasium and voted for the same candidate. The gym was aptly named the Black precinct, and as election returns were announced on the radio that night, the Black precinct was often the swing vote.

If anyone should doubt the importance of community gathering at the one Black school in the community, fast forward to the 1970s. Mandatory integration of all schools in the little rural town was ordered. The Black school was changed to a

© KONINKLIJKE BRILL NV, LEIDEN, 2018 | DOI 10.1163/9789004378735_008

middle school, and the city ordered the immediate demolition of the gymnasium at that school.

Even though the gym had recently been renovated with new floors, locker rooms, and a new stage, the gym was the only building on the campus that was razed to the ground. The voting district lines were redrawn and the Black vote was sprinkled among four other districts. The power of the Black vote ended in the dust and rubble of the demolished community meeting place.

The Black leaders and one Black principal of the segregated school system where I grew up really only wanted one thing – equitable resources. They wanted books that did not fall apart in the children's hands. They wanted resources that were not used for a decade by white schools and then passed on to the Black children after the white schools received updated resources. They wanted equal resources. A sense of community fuelled the pride and confidence that the all Black faculty could educate the kids adequately.

Children were taught by teachers who lived in the community and attended the same churches and gatherings as the parents. Discipline problems or poor grades were discussed across church pews on Sunday mornings and handled immediately. The instantaneous correction given to the guilty child was often punctuated by the statement: "I know you didn't just make me shame in front of all the church! Don't you ever! Wait until I get you home!"

Black parents petitioned for equal resources for their schools and communities, not necessarily for integration. Schools were taught by teachers with a vested interest in improving lives of children who would re-enter the community as adult citizens. However, what they got was far more than equal resources and it continues to gather momentum into the present day where white flight, followed closely by middle class Black flight, has resulted in segregated cities.

When I left my small rural town, and moved to the capital city in the 1980s, I lived in an inner-city school zone because my resources would not allow me to live on the outskirts. By the time my children were school-aged, I knew that they could not attend the school located two blocks from my home. The school had rapidly deteriorated into a state that echoed our surroundings.

The school offered few extracurriculars, there were no magnet or technology courses, and the buildings were dilapidated, outdated, and in general disrepair. All the new modern schools were constructed on the outskirts of town in the more affluent white neighbourhoods. Every time a new neighbourhood was developed away from the inner city, a new elementary, middle, and high school were also constructed within walking distance for the white students.

I simply could not afford to move to the enrollment lines of any of the new suburban schools. I had to make the system work to my advantage without moving. That is when I began to enroll my children in magnet programs, minority to majority transfers, and in the case of my youngest, the gifted program.

Unlike the obvious absence of police presence in my segregated school, the integrated schools of my children with a high population of Black students had a constant presence of at least one law enforcement officer on campus at all times. That way, my children were afforded the same opportunities as the more affluent white population without my having to move to a better neighbourhood. My children never attended neighbourhood schools.

My son was placed in one magnet program or another, depending on the location of the school. If it was a fully funded, higher-scoring school, then he was enrolled in the magnet. My daughter attended magnet programs until middle school, when after much research into the system's middle schools, I decided that the magnet component was not going to work for me this time. I still did not live in the suburbs yet and attending the neighbourhood school was out of the question. Therefore, I had her tested for the gifted program in fifth grade and she became a member of the most segregated school-within-a-school program to date.

But how did my neighbourhood become the keeper of inferior school sources? With the enactment of integration, white parents who could afford to leave the inner city left and took with them the resources and tax dollars necessary to segregate themselves in another part of town. The strong block vote of the Black community was decimated and the school board and city council were run almost exclusively by white men.

They decided how to spend tax dollars and the decisions to build newer and better schools in the suburbs became normal. What could we, the Black community say? The law did not exclude us from attending the better and fully funded schools in the suburbs. Many mortgage companies broke the law and used redline tactics to make Black families believe they couldn't afford to live in white suburbs. Personally, we were simply financially unable to relocate in mass numbers to these schools.

What happened to Black spending power? Back in the time of segregation, Blacks were only allowed to live in one area of town. Most families were too poor to afford cars and had to walk everywhere. Black-owned businesses were patronized and allowed to flourish.

Groceries and other staples were purchased from Black grocery stores located within the community. Black-owned building contractors did all the construction work for the Black community. Electricians, plumbers and other maintenance workers were also Black community members.

In essence, the community took care of itself by investing money into businesses that in turn invested it back into the community. Once integration was put into full effect, part of community power was also phased out. Black citizens had mobility and were granted entrance into white establishments and sadly chose to take more resources into the white establishments.

Before integration, Black schools were obviously providing a quality education in spite of limited resources. Many prominent leaders and world-renowned advocates have risen to power after receiving degrees from segregated all-Black school systems. The request for equal resources was just a venture in the direction of making the Black school system even better. However, instead of equal resources, the community got integration and a snowball effect that has yet to stop building momentum.

What has caused this snowball effect? Essentially, the sentiments of segregationists have not changed in today's society. White flight continues to occur in significant numbers from the public-school system, especially in inner city schools. Integration allowed middle and upper middle-class families to move away from the segregated communities so prevalent in the 1950s and diluted the Black voting clout of the "block vote."

White businesses gained more access to Black money as Blacks were no longer shunned in the uptown establishment and *coloured only entrances*. As a result, the once prominent Black owned businesses have decreased and many have simply shut down. Those who participated in white flight did not just move to the suburbs and remain. Remember, the mindset of the segregationist remained steadfast.

Therefore, when more affluent Blacks move into the newer neighbourhoods, many who participate in white flight have retreated even further to the edge of city limits and in some cases left the city altogether. In a more extreme action, the white population has attempted to use its political clout and tax base to carve out a mini-city on the edge of town that completely destroy the structure of the inner city.

Presently, I am living in one of those many suburbs on the outskirts of the city. I often return to my hometown and traverse the many neighbourhoods and paths that nurtured me through my youth. I was educated in the segregated Black school in the sixties for grades 1–6 and in the integrated school system for grades 7–12. As my education progressed, I found that the vigilant schooling of the Black teachers I encountered in my early years of schooling were what allowed me to navigate college successfully.

It was never about the lack of ability to educate our own, it was truly about the resources. In my hometown, all the old businesses that once flourished are long gone. The slab from the gymnasium that stood as the epicentre of the Black community is still perched on the corner of what was once the only Black school in the city. When my grandchildren visit me in Baton Rouge, I will take them to the old neighbourhood to see the house where their father was born and the neighbourhood where he grew up.

We will make this journey, however, in the daylight. Everyone knows that you do not go into that particular neighbourhood at night. I do not believe that people who have the means should not move on to better lives once they have the ability to do so, but education is a constant in this equation. The school system has a responsibility to maintain equality, no matter the neighbourhood in which it abides.

A flourishing school system promotes good neighbourhoods. White flight from the Baton Rouge schools left a wasteland of once flourishing schools. I am inclined to believe that after decades of marches, suffering, lawsuits, and legislation, the forefathers could not possibly have imagined that the request for equal resources would one day become the fallout of integration.

ARIEL QUINIO

9. THE CONTESTED NEW TERRITORY

Integration and Dissatisfaction

Grounded on critical perspectives, the individual and institutional factors contributing to the unequal employment opportunities in a large urban center are explored to challenge the existing policies on immigration and employment of the Internationally Educated Professionals (IEPs). With the goal of promoting a more equitable social integration of racialized individuals from diverse communities, I reflect on narratives according to the employment experiences of IEPs. The parallels connecting the narratives reveal hierarchical power relations. The emerging theme mainly suggests the employers' bias for the perpetuation of norms in the employment hiring practices anchored on postcolonial white supremacy and native English speakers' ideology.

The increasing arrivals of immigrants in many countries recently has reached an unprecedented proportion. Many government leaders and policy-makers are caught in limbo at resolving one of the most controversial issues of the modern era. The implication that wealthy nations are safe havens for immigrant workers is contested based on the realities revealed in the narratives of immigrants. The influx of immigrants to the Global North from various domains often results in contradictions with the dominant culture, generating complexities in labour market integration and employment success of IEPs.

The term *Internationally Educated Professionals* refers, in the case of my research to foreign-trained immigrants who entered Canada in the Greater Toronto Area (GTA) from 1988–2008 under the economic class category of the immigration policy. The narratives focusing on employment experiences of IEPs are emotionally-laden and situated in the context of the changing policy landscape, fluctuating economic conditions, and the increasing trends of globalization and migration.

The immigration policies and programs in Canada are replete with provisions that integrate all immigrant workers in the mainstream socioeconomic arena. Building on the ideals of multiculturalism, there is an existing policy ensemble that aimed in assisting immigrants to overcome employment barriers. Whereas there are increasing government-initiated policies designed to assist foreign-trained immigrants in finding employment in their intended professions, many IEPs are overrepresented in low skilled jobs regardless of their credentials.

© KONINKLIJKE BRILL NV, LEIDEN, 2018 | DOI 10.1163/9789004378735_009

The most recurring problems related to the integration of IEPs have been the regulatory barriers imposed upon them by the Canadian federal and provincial governments; namely, the re-assessment of their foreign credentials and the problem of their integration to the cultures of practice in Canada. The policy that foreign-trained immigrants are ready to step up in the labour market is actually very misleading.

Results of the study indicate that most of the IEPs are indeed not ready yet to step into skilled jobs as they normally have to undergo years of re-credentialing processes. As many of the IEPs in this study have experienced, they have undergone a long process of re-credentialing procedures upon their arrival to integrate in their profession. This is regardless of the strict evaluation of the IEPs' qualifications which they have already been subjected prior to their immigration.

The *Canadian experience requirement* has been considered as part of the realities of the IEPs' employment seeking experiences as in the case of Sindhu, an African-Somalian who arrived to Canada in 1992. Sindhu had spent more than five years of seeking employment in his intended profession as a medical doctor but ended up only working as a general labourer in a warehouse company. When interviewed as to what took him so long to seek and find employment in Canada since his arrival, he replied:

> ... the biggest problem was many employers did not recognize my foreign credentials. It's very hard. When I came here, how come employers were asking for my Canadian experience when I was very new in this country? ... wherever I go, they asked for Canadian experience.

Sindhu reveals a striking reality on what constitutes as a major barrier among IEPs in finding employment in their intended profession. He found his first job in Canada as a general labourer in a warehouse after five years of unsuccessful employment seeking experiences.

As a general labourer, he pointed out many negative attributes of his working environment including the asymmetrical power relation between workers and management who always exerts pressures to their subordinates through rigid company rules, higher production and unrealistic work expectations and demands. He realized that this nature of employment does not help him to get any closer to his profession as a medical doctor. Being dismayed with these unpleasant experiences, he went back and forth to his home country where he continued practicing his medical career but never in Canada.

Joe was a system engineer from the Philippines who came to Canada in 2001. Accordingly, he came to Canada as a professional and he paid large amount of money to the Canadian immigration to assess his qualifications. Joe explained that he should not come to Canada, if in the first place, he was found unfit for the Canadian labour market based on his assessment results.

Joe seeks answers to his two questions: "Where is the job in my intended profession that they promised me I could find in Canada? Why they're asking for my Canadian experience when in fact they assessed me already?" These two questions he raised can be interpreted within the discourses of trust and mistrust between the IEPs and the Canadian immigration system. Results revealed that only when the IEPs arrived in Canada that they came to realize the difficulties of finding jobs particularly in their field of specialization. Joe rationalizes this reality when he said:

> I worked in many different companies just for me to gain a Canadian experience. I have worked in the factory to support my family. But I really didn't like it. In my first job [as a general labourer], my coworkers passed on to me all the dirty jobs that no one would like to accept. I was like doing, a sort of … jack-of-all-trades.

The most evident manifestation of the *Canadian experience requirement* as a barrier in the employment among the IEPs was observed in Rose's employment seeking in one of the companies she applied in after her arrival to Canada in 2002. Rose, another Filipino IEP who is now a Certified General Accountant (CGA) tells her ordeal on the Canadian experience requirement as follows:

> There was a time I almost get hired after passing through a series of interviews, and they offered me the job. There was already a contract to be signed in front of me, but still they delayed. After a week, I received a phone call. They told me that they're retracting the job offer and the contract. It was a big punch on my face …!

Clearly, the reason why Rose's offer of employment was retracted is because of her lack of Canadian experience considering that she was then very new in Canada and that the employer preferred job candidates with a Canadian experience. The employer's action that favoured job candidates with native Canadian backgrounds is apparently an expression of mistrust to an IEP with foreign credentials.

With the most recent immigration policies, the ability to communicate in spoken English has continuously become an important factor in the integration of IEPs. Language barrier has been observed in the case of Li, an immigrant from Hong Kong who initially could not find employment in her field as a former bank financial analyst because of her distinctive Chinese accent. During the interview, Li revealed:

> In Canada, you don't start right away in a higher position…. I first worked as a waitress in a fast food restaurant and as a part-time cashier in a grocery store. I didn't like my first job here so I went back to Hong Kong.

The role of language in the integration of IEPs as non-native-English speakers (NNES) is more evident in the cases of two occasional teachers, namely, Grace, a Filipino and Vlad, an Eastern European. Based on their employment experiences, the role of language was crystal-clear in their attempts to be integrated in the mainstream teaching profession. The narrative of Grace was part of her employment seeking experiences when she was applying to become a teacher. The school principal who was interviewing her had abruptly ended up her interview in favour of other applicants who were lined up outside. In this experience, Grace recalled:

I was not yet finished answering the questions. But … I felt like the interviewer
was already pushing me out of the door in favour of other job candidates …
I felt like I came from a different planet.

The discourse of being treated as a different member of the profession on the basis
of language or accent is also true in the case of Vlad who despite of being a certified
teacher continuously struggles in finding a permanent teaching job for more than 10
years now as he explained in his interview extract:

They said my English is NOT very good …
But how about my MATH?
… I'm a Math teacher, and for us/
the language issue should be taken separately.
I was not [trained] to speak [like] Shakespeare//
… [but] Math is a universal language.

Vlad's experiences resonate more of the employment seeking experiences as
presented in the case of Grace who is in the same field of teaching. The main
argument in Vlad's case was that he cannot get a permanent teaching position and
he was critical of the ambiguity that he experienced in the hiring of NNES teachers.

The narratives offered an explanation to what has been called as the '*double
standard assessment*' of the IEPs' credentials representing the nature of reality that
Vlad called it '*a foul play*' and '*a waste of their time and money.*' On the other hand,
Rose described her experience as '*a punch on her face*' when her job offer and
contract was retracted by her prospective employer because of her being a newcomer
and lack of Canadian experience. The non-recognition of professional backgrounds
among the IEPs in Canada had caused Rose to pursue the re-certification of her
credentials that took her five long years of study to get her CGA designation.

Employment experiences of foreign-trained immigrants in the host society are not
so inclusive. A complex reality suggests that IEPs were not being treated with the same
respect as non-IEPs in the area of employment access and opportunities in their field of
expertise. The vulnerabilities among IEPs in precarious jobs can be disheartening that
they are like digging their own grave leading to a dead-end career as in Sindhu's case.
There is a number of IEPs who have navigated a curvature employment trajectory
and have been integrated but dissatisfied with their jobs because of lower designation,
non-permanent jobs and invisible barriers to job promotion.

The source of dissatisfaction among the IEPs can be traced from the fact that their
distinctive identities were contested by the dominant society. Results suggest that the
challenges they had been facing can be attributed to certain individual factors such
as ethnicity, linguistic and cultural differences. Moreover, institutional factors of the
workplace such as exclusion among IEPs within the community of practice have
established and sustained domination, subordination, and marginalization.

DERRICK ROBINSON

10. CRANES, CONES, AND INVISIBLE WALLS

How Zip codes, Economic Development, and
Housing Patterns Strengthen Segregation

The modern urban centre is a product of more than 70 years of economic and racial segregation in America. Economic and racial segregation, particularly in housing, makes disparities increasingly visible. Poor and middle class became increasingly synonymous with Black and White, respectively. The distribution of resources in the emerging modern era has become reliant on three criteria: (a) race, (b) income, and (c) educational attainment.

The last two decades of gentrification in urban centres have continued the tradition. Today, one's zip code can determine one's trajectory. Zip codes can set groups on an intergenerational cycle that impacts educational experiences, outlook, and options. This chapter discusses how economic development and the location of resources impacts economic segregation and its hidden costs on Black, resource-deprived people.

This chapter also suggests that racial and economic segregation has created *invisible walls* in the modern urban centre. Unlike typical discussions on segregation, this chapter examines segregation through information found within zip codes of urban centres. This chapter closes with a brief discussion on the impact of cranes, cones, and invisible walls on the modern urban centre.

Cranes and Cones are a symbol of economic development. *Cranes*, machines designed to lift and lower materials during construction, and *cones*, orange pylons used to ensure road safety during construction, indicate the desire to spend money to improve, or grow, an area. The decision on how to engage in *cranes and cones* is dependent on two concepts: (a) *Effort and Demand*, and (b) *Government and Private Business Relationships*. Effort and demand is about the assignment of value through action.

Since money is limited, economic development tells the public where and what the developer values, or expends its effort. *Demand* depends heavily in research and knowledge of consumer tastes, preferences, and desire to spend. The presence of cranes and cones is a statement of value and belief in the people where the development is taking place. The location of businesses in distinct areas, regardless of urban area, can represent either superior research or the presence of bias.

Bias in economic development reveals assumptions about consumer preferences based on developer opinions or values, rather than local research. This chapter will use the company Panera Bread, known for its artisan bread, sandwiches and soups,

© KONINKLIJKE BRILL NV, LEIDEN, 2018 | DOI 10.1163/9789004378735_010

and its general atmosphere, as a symbol for effort and demand. Beyond food, Panera Bread is easily observed as a place where groups of people socialize.

Cranes and cones represent direct and indirect relationships between government and private business. Cranes and cones are not accidental decisions and, in many cases, are not evenly distributed. The construction of malls, shopping centres, office buildings, or restaurants are the direct relationships of increasing consumer access to goods and services. Should this relationship only result in economic development for a distinct group/community, that group becomes increasingly *resource-advantaged* over time.

Modern urban centres appear to have *invisible walls* that represent a dividing line between people based upon their social, economic, and racial association. The invisible wall is a symbolic product of habit and institution. As a habit, adhering to the invisible wall is supported in the daily patterns of one's existence. Adults, for example, go to work and then home in a predictable fashion, stopping at places that are convenient for them and their pattern.

Adults learn to incorporate the resources near them into their lifestyle, reducing the need to venture outside of their community. As these habits become shared by people on both sides of the wall, they become institutionalized. As Person A knows not to encroach upon into Person B's community, Person B accepts that Person A does not belong in Person B's community, and vice versa. When governmental and business developers only choose to engage in cranes and cones in Person B's community, Person A becomes *resource-deprived* over time.

ZIP CODES

Given the integration of cranes and cones and invisible walls, zip codes allow us to identify which areas experience either resource-deprivation or resource-advantage. Utilizing the store locator map on the Panera Bread company website www.panereabread.com for each respective city, zip codes were selected in areas that stores were located and in areas where they were not. Five zip codes were selected per city. Utilizing the website www.city-data.com, information on race (expressed as the percent of White residents), median income, and educational attainment (expressed as the percent of people with a Bachelor's degree or higher) was retrieved for analysis of four selected cities that represent varying densities of urban centres: (a) Charlotte, NC., (b) Chicago, Il., (c) Dallas, TX., and (d) New York City, NY. Through examining twenty zip-codes in four urban areas, it can be argued that there is a strong correlation between zip code residence and race, median income, and educational attainment. There is also an observed strong direct relationship between zip code characteristics and effort and demand.

Charlotte and Chicago: Near Perfect Strong Segregation

Both the cities of Charlotte and Chicago displayed very strong relationships (between .65 and 1.00) between all variables. For Charlotte, the relationship

40

between Zip Code and Effort and Demand was perfectly positive. This suggests that are directly connected to economic development. Closely behind for Charlotte are the relationships between Median Income and Educational Attainment (.999), Zip Code and Race (.989), and Effort and Demand and Race (.989). This suggests that Charlotte has high levels of racial and economic segregation.

Like Charlotte, the city of Chicago has high levels of segregation, with Zip-Code and Effort and Demand being perfectly positive (1.00). This suggest that some zip-code may not be as valued when it comes to economic development. Race has a strong relationship with Median Income (.995) and Educational Attainment (.994). This suggests high disparities in access to education and financial resources based related to race.

New York City: Strongly Segregated

While not as segregated as Charlotte and Chicago, New York City does have strong correlations between all categories, except Median Income and Effort and Demand (.634). Race is most strongly related to Educational Attainment (.996), but not as strongly related to Effort and Demand. New York's Zip Code 11101, for example, represents a more racially diverse environment that has experienced economic development. Effort and Demand and Zip-code (.667), although strongly related, is near moderate levels.

Dallas: Moderately Strong Segregation

Dallas is strongly segregated in many areas, primarily economic and educational. Zip-code is strongly related to Median Income (.989) and Educational Attainment (.936). This suggests significant segregation related to wealth and education. While Effort and Demand are only moderately related to Zip-code (.408) and Median Income (.523), it has a strong relation to Race (.926). This suggests that race may trump money and education when it comes to economic development.

CONCLUSION

This observation of the impact of cranes, cones, and invisible walls suggests that racial and economic segregation creates structurally different life experiences for the resource-deprived and the resource-advantaged within the same city. These life experiences are not always the product of individual choice. They can be the product of effort, demand, and the economic development choices made by government and private industry.

What is observed in cranes and cones and the invisible walls that they help to create carry heavy implications for the value of lives. Outsiders look upon these resource-deprived areas and form value-statements and opinions of the people there. They assume that the resource-deprived do not want any better or, worse yet, chose

41

to be resource-deprived. Outsiders fail to see, the hidden hands of government and business that hide in plain sight.

These zip-codes, as invisible walls, impact schooling experiences, social outlook, and awareness of options. Teachers, in the age of accountability, elect not to teach in areas they believe are resource-deprived for beliefs that students do not want to learn and fear that student performance may reflect on them. As a result, schools in resource-deprived areas often find a cadre of barely-qualified teachers who bring a disposition of failure and negativity to the classroom. This observed phenomenon also impacts how individuals are served and protected.

Law enforcement police communities with containment policies based on fear and hatred. The shooting of Terrance Crutcher in Tulsa, Oklahoma, where one officer from a helicopter refers to Crutcher as looking like a *bad dude*, serves as an example of the fear. Law enforcement hyper-masculinization of teens and pre-teens, noticed in the describing of 12-year-old Tamir Rice as being possibly 20 years old, places black children in danger in resource-deprived areas. To address this observation, intentional effort must be provided from governmental stakeholders who can directly reverse economic and racial segregation based influenced by zip-code.

RECOMMENDATIONS

As government and business are intentionally, or unintentionally, responsible for cranes, cones, and invisible walls, solutions must emerge from them to resolve these conditions. Where voting may appear to be the necessary step, voting alone, as have been done, will not help. Replacing the same disposition in a different suit will not resolve this crisis.

Preparing and promoting candidates who have a disposition of service and a keen understanding of the impact of zip code politics is a recommended first step in reversing the effects of cranes, cones, and invisible walls. Preparing and promoting mayors, police chiefs, city councils, school superintendents, and departments of commerce officials who have the mind, heart, and ears for resource-deprived people begins the gradual process of redirecting the values behind cranes, cones, and invisible walls.

SHARON D. JONES-EVERSLEY, DIANE M. HARNEK HALL
AND JACQUELINE M. RHODEN-TRADER

11. FIGHTING THE POWERS THAT BE

*Examining Conflicting Dual Legitimate Powers
Operative in Urban America*

It's a hard knock life for us, is a lyric from *Annie.* The lyric symbolizes the social-political contractarianism lens used to examine America's failed social contract with urban communities. *Contractarianism* is operationalized as the governing constructs and legitimate power that regulate societal norms in urban communities. While Annie and her orphaned peers are fictional characters, their failed social contract with the government and their community mirrors the polarizing relative deprivation and social disability realities of many urban communities.

Sandtown-Winchester is a Baltimore neighbourhood; this neighbourhood was home to Freddie Gray, Jr., a 25-year-old Black male, who died while in police custody in 2015. The community is one that provides a context for contractarianism. Legitimate power is a positional power that hierarchically affects communities' social, political, public health, economic and environmental infrastructures via its authority, influence, persistence and effectiveness.

This chapter explores the legal and illegal legitimate powersoperative in Sandtown. From a social-political perspective, legal legitimate power exemplifies the communal role of politicians, policy makers, police and community leaders; illegal legitimate power epitomizes the influential role of drug dealers, gang leaders, human traffickers and corrupt legal power in urban communities.

Baltimore City's social contract has repeatedly failed it for decades. Sandtown-Winchester, a 72-block community in West Baltimore exceeds Maryland in majority of the poor well-being categories (i.e., poverty, infant mortality, crime, vacant homes, etc.). Coupled with their frustration with the dual legitimate powers, these poor living conditions result in an emotional, physical, social and socioeconomic state of relative deprivation. Sandtown residents are angered by their poor quality of life, denied access to resources from legal legitimate powers and ongoing oppression from illegal legitimate power. Sandtown has become a socially disabled community. The social disability stabilizes the community's relative deprivation while corroding any sustainable progress.

Caught in the complex web between the legal and illegal legitimate powers are the urban community leaders. They are unsung indigenous forerunners of the legitimate power who continuously advocate for Sandtown's welfare. Selected by default because few accept the challenging role of fighting with the contradicting

© KONINKLIJKE BRILL NV, LEIDEN, 2018 | DOI 10.1163/9789004378735_011

legitimate powers. These community leaders live in Sandtown, and witness firsthand the devastating impact of relative deprivation and social disability. Efforts to address Baltimore's failed social contract are complicated by embezzlement, racketeering, brutality and drug trafficking; that is they are made complicated by illegal legitimate power, not legal legitimate power. The litany of indictments includes the former City's Mayor, Comptroller, council persons, police, correction officers and community leaders. Indigenous leaders still press forward to contend with drug dealers, gangs, human traffickers and the corrupt legal legitimate power. Urban America's indigenous leaders' sacrifices, intelligence and negotiation capacities are too often undervalued or ignored by the legal legitimate powers.

Sandtown, is a distressed neighbourhood like many in America. The community experiences high-poverty (over 50% of household incomes under $25,000), high arrest rates (the highest rate of residents in jails and prisons of all Baltimore neighbourhoods), high juvenile arrest rates (over 200 per 1,000 residents), high infant mortality rates (over 20 in 1,000 live births); and high teen birth rates (over 100 in 1,000 residents). Statistics like these often draw attention for change from policy makers and Sandtown is no exception.

During the 1990's, over $100 million was directed toward re-gentrification and community improvement efforts. Unfortunately, the data demonstrates the amount of money intended for change did not spur promised, changes for families. In fact, it has proven difficult to determine how exactly all that money was spent and, even more so, to link it to realized improvements.

When distrust of those who make and enforce laws is present, the need for security is shifted to a more viable source. Gangs take advantage of this need. Gangs provide a source of identity critical to subcultures that have created their own laws and social systems. So, to identify with a gang can, in many cases, be less dangerous than not.

With high arrest and incarceration rates for juveniles and adults and the likely prospects of hostile interactions with police, young people have cultivated a fatalistic perspective of their futures. They are willing to risk joining a gang to develop an image, engage with peers, escape difficult circumstances and make some gains before their freedom, possessions, and, considering the likelihood of injury and death for drug dealers, their lives are taken away.

High juvenile arrest rates enculturate youth to the drudgery of arrest and incarceration. Further these experiences expose youth to who may be more heavily involved in gangs and drugs. Juvenile incarceration disrupts the educational trajectory for youth and fulfils a schema of the hard times many of the adults around them endure.

With more than 50% of high school students absent more than 20 school days a year in Sandtown, essential socialization to work and college is diverted, giving community gangs an entire to socialize youth to the subculture and perpetuate it. Typically, young people know older relatives and peers in gangs who use natural adolescent tendencies to join groups and persuade them to join. Music, movies, and a range of media images that glamorize the perils of street life normalize activities typical for gangs and motivate youth to experience them.

Dealing drugs is a business and gangs are the corporate structure. They have recruiting, marketing, pricing, manufacturing, distribution, pay roll ... just like any legitimate business. Although there are not cubicles or departments within these corporations, street corners are a familiar enclave where transactions are made. This corporate climate is more conducive to prospective positions for many youth than sterile offices with strange job titles.

Gangs have established themselves in neighbourhoods like Sandtown. They are a part of the fabric of community life and provide leadership in business and partnerships. After the riots, gang leaders assisted in the recovery. They have created illegal legitimate power that is influential by keeping their promises of supplying jobs, drugs, and camaraderie of membership.

Just over 600,000 call Baltimore home. Amidst the esthetically pleasing views of its Inner Harbor, historic Federal Hill, Fort McHenry, are dilapidated buildings, low performing schools, pockets of poverty, grime and a plethora of crime and neighborhoods resembling West Baltimore's Sandtown-Winchester neighborhood. Like any criminal enterprise, supply and demand dictates success or failure, and human traffic yields upwards of 40 billion dollars annually, suggesting great demand.

The forced prostitution of women and children who are trafficked requires unique law enforcement response. The phenomenon and its response have major implications for victims. The failure of law enforcement officers to properly screen and identify victims of human trafficking when they make arrests and detain them, further victimizes individuals who are coerced into criminal activities.

As the fastest growing criminal enterprise in the world, and second most profitable, human trafficking is thriving in the United States and around the world. Across Maryland, human trafficking for sex or labor occurs more often than the general populous realizes. Its proximity to byways and throughways such as the Interstate 95 corridor which links New York City, Philadelphia and Washington D.C. has numerous truck stops and bus stations that place high demand on sex trafficking, as businesses are disguised as legal enterprises.

Human trafficking has long been a social problem in Baltimore. As Maryland's largest city, neighborhoods like Sandtown are suitable targets for human trafficking rings to establish themselves. Legal and illegal legitimate powers are contributing factors. The blight, high number of single family headed households, low educational attainment provides great yield of victims for traffickers.

Like most criminal enterprises, human trafficking requires complicity with law enforcement (police, judges and government officials). The very entities charged with serving and protecting become law violators by assisting, participating in or turning a blind eye to human trafficking. Of major concern in human trafficking is despite its prevalence, most victims are never identified and perpetrators are rarely convicted. Corruption within the criminal justice system at all levels makes human trafficking possible. On the legal end is the Maryland Human Trafficking Taskforce which aims to toughen laws against human trafficking. Two bills stiffening the penalties for human trafficking have been passed since 2014. On the programmatic end is the Samaritan Women, Maryland's first long-term residential program for victims of domestic human trafficking. Located near Sandtown the organization provides restoration residential care for up to 14 survivors in the form of counseling services for factors such as childhood sexual abuse, fatherlessness, poverty, neglect, substance abuse and subsequent sex trafficking victimization.

Illegal legitimate powers include gang and drug culture, which are historically strong in Sandtown. Although not widespread in this community, the government's complicity in human trafficking is based on its high profit margins, judges' acceptance of bribes by drug kingpins and the treatment of victims as criminals. The 2015 case of teen victims taken from their Sandtown neighborhood with computer-aided technology and trafficked to Baltimore County is just a microcosm of the larger sex trafficking epidemic that permeates America's urban communities.

Policy initiatives like more policing, zero tolerance, affordable housing, school improvement etc. are powerful legal legitimate promises that have not been realized. Powerful illegal legitimate entities have filled in the gaps left by these failed initiatives. In the absence of legitimate promises, the illegitimate ones provide and sustain the inevitable futures of those living in communities like Sandtown. There is distrust among residents. Living in desolate neighbourhoods with high crime rates and abandoned buildings many do not feel that their plight is understood or that positive change is possible or intended. Those in leadership roles have little power to engage with policy makers or outright avoid anyone in the government due to their distrust, previous arrests, or involvement in illegal activities.

These neighbourhoods harbor residents who are in pain. Many who work hard to provide a household income, get an education, and raise a family, are treated with the same bated scepticism as criminals by police. Because of their address, many report having been falsely arrested. Many report having suffered great losses due to injuries and deaths of family and friends. When illegal legitimate power wins out over legitimate power, the paths to legitimate success become difficult to find and interactions within the community with legitimate power are tainted. Instead, avenues to the influential illegal legitimate power are simply more accessible. These powerful influences held by gangs have effectively sustained the community over time.

Yes, living in Sandtown is a *hard knock life*. Unlike the fictional characters in *Annie*, relative deprivation and social disability exist. In Urban America, illegal legitimate power has the status quo advantage, and its authority, influence, persistence and effectiveness far exceeds the legal legitimate power.

Decades of generational poverty, health disparities, institutional racism and systemic inequities have become Urban America's social norm. However, these social norms are not normal; they are inhumane. Urban communities are socially disabled hostages caught between the complex conflicting legitimate powers. Immediate legal legitimate actions are warranted to protect and uphold America's social contract with Urban America. Relative deprivation and social disability anywhere in America threatens the safety, health and welfare of all America.

DERRICK D. MCKISICK

12. THE DECREASING VALUE OF LABOR IN THE MODERN AGE BROKEN PROMISE

Black Deaths and Blue Ribbons

The United States (U.S.) capitalist system is predicated on value. Each element of society has a relative value compared to something else, but as with most things, in our increasingly global community, the value of life continues to decline. With the continued diminution of labour, life, itself, is under assault. In the two preceding centuries, the value of labour helped to elevate every person in society.

Even in marginalized, disadvantaged, and segregated communities, the value of labour provided these communities with a certain measure of security, safety, and stability. With globalization, and increasing amounts of automation and artificial intelligence, protection of life has become increasingly less important because labour is no longer a finite commodity necessary for the continuation of capitalism. This new reality, as the 21st century continues to unfold, increases the importance of scarce resources.

The fight to maintain control of finite economic, political, and cultural resources has speeded the process of marginalization among all groups in U.S. society. Several events have marked this change in focus and intensified acrimony between groups vying for portions of an increasingly smaller economic pie. The Black Lives Matter (BLM), Charleston church shooting, and presidential election of 2016 epitomize these rapid changes. New contested spaces highlighted in this modern context have exposed the ragged underpinnings of a system that no longer is required to protect life because life, increasingly, is less necessary for labour.

When the death of Trevon Martin occurred, there was an explosion across newspaper headlines, television newscast, and radio talk shows. Martin's death forced U.S. citizens to confront the realities of racial injustice that still plague U.S. communities. The killing of an unarmed African-American teen and acquittal of an armed neighbourhood watch leader ripped away the band aid of the so-called post-racial U.S., which had been heralded widely with the election of President Obama.

In the chaos that ensued, BLM was born. This movement placed a simple proposition before the entire United States that Black Live Matters, too. It highlighted the seeming incongruity of a nation dedicated to the protection of every life to a perceived disregard or ambivalence about the importance of African American lives. With each new incident between law enforcement and African Americans across the

United States, with each athlete kneeling during the playing of the national anthem, and with each act of civil disobedience, BLM has refused to allow these events to fade from the U.S. political discussion.

The position of BLM relative to the treatment of African Americans and their relationship with the law enforcement community continues to resonate across the United States. The value of labour has been eroded in society, leaving many cities, which had been the centre of production, without the need for labour. The lack of employment opportunities has left historically marginalized communities with few options to gain a fair hearing for their grievances.

Additionally, racial discrimination continues to marginalize African Americans. Higher unemployment, incarceration, and dropout rates continue to plague African American communities. These outcomes, in addition to the lack of educational advancement, create a difficult outlook for these already economically, politically, and socially periphery communities. The lack of full employment and education limits efforts to address local issues and force local political leaders, who control law enforcement, to address their concerns relative to policing African American communities.

On June 17, 2015, Dylann Roof attended a church service at Emanuel African Methodist Episcopal Church located in Charleston, South Carolina. Roof, an avowed white supremacist, assassinated nine people. This shooting sent shockwaves through the United States. An intentional shooting at a church, known as a centre of African-American activism in Charleston, highlights a far deeper attack aimed at the heart of African American independence and resistance.

The African-American church continues to be the single entity African Americans control in U.S. society. Historically, churches, church services, and church community functions offered an opportunity for African Americans to organize to resist enslavement, segregation, and oppression. These multi-faceted aspects of the African American church create a place for a community to function and provide support for various activities.

The symbolic nature of an attack on the nine parishioners at Emanuel African Methodist Episcopal Church struck a violent blow against African American engagement. The event revealed the uneasiness of people seeking to maintain their traditional hold on the depleting resources reserved for people in marginalized communities. White supremacist shootings and police shootings of unarmed citizens leaves local citizens and the entire U.S. to ponder the nature of racially motivated violence. These activities have failed, however, to explore the implications of the economic reality. Continued arguments for and against BLM mask important changes that protest, political action, and community groups must address.

The shrinking social, economic, and cultural resources of the United States continue to be strained with the increasing amount of globalization. Around the globe, the development of a truly world market has placed different groups of labour in direct competition and applies more pressure in each country that participates in the world market. Transportation and communication provide new avenues for countries to engage in trade.

Where there had been limits in the conduct of trade between nations, the constraints have been removed to create a more connected global market. Money, investment, and capitalism continue to transform relationships between nations. As countries around the world develop, the United States faces more competition in a much smaller marketplace, a space where labour is not as important as it once was.

These developments have led to the continued deindustrialization of the United States, placing greater burdens on the strained resources local, state, and federal governments, families, private charities, and middle-class households. The ability of lower middle and upper lower-class workers to provide the financial support necessary to give their children a better life continues to erode in today 's economic climate. This new climate increases pressure on all areas of the U.S. economy to address these changing needs.

The presidential election of 2016 provided a window to view the raging class discontent among different groups of U.S. citizens. People formerly belonging to the middle class, who struggle to maintain class status, participated in the election to address their economic distress. As these changes continue to undercut their social, economic, and political opportunities, the arguments of Democratic and Republican candidates avoided discussing the hidden costs of the changing economic and labour environment.

When politicians promised to stem the tide of job losses, they failed to mention the quantum leaps companies are making in the development of artificial intelligence systems and automation as culprits in the battle to secure finite resources. While politicians continue use immigration, racism, affirmative action, and stereotyping to further the political agenda, they failed to identify how these systems can be used to further destabilize human labour markets. The failure to acknowledge these systems weakens all aspects of American society and places a larger wedge between the American public and capitalism.

American companies and politicians continue to ignore or to equivocate about the changes in the allocation of finite resources. Without an awareness of these new factors, American citizens will continue to battle for economic advancement, but with no real understanding of why the economic and labour systems are no longer sustainable. The promise of restoring an older political, social, and economic order based on the same formula of racial divisions and class discontent, without acknowledging this new reality, fails to create an opportunity for all groups to address this new future that is taking shape before our eyes.

These new systems coupled with globalization have the ability to revolutionize the ways we live, work, and engage with each other and the outside world. While developments promise more autonomy and freedom, they also create an environment where human labour becomes less and less necessary. As human labour becomes less and less vital, the protection of human life will become less and less important.

Labour has been the most important component in the development of the U.S. providing fuel necessary to power American industrial expansion through 20th century. Immigration, urbanization, and mechanization have served as cornerstones of U.S. business, political, and economic success. As the 21st century unfolds, the effective use of technology has the potential to create an entirely new way of life. As businesses implement these new money-saving and labour-saving strategies, how will they impact the American worker? How do these new systems complement or complicate cultural, political, and economic organization in the United States?

American political parties have to engage in the larger issues rather than continuing to participate in the politics of discord and rage that seek to exploit superficial differences for political gain. So far political and social arguments merely scratch the surface of the great impact that technology continues to have on the U.S. capitalist system. BLM, the Charleston church shooting, the presidential election of 2016 provide simplistic contexts to the evolving re-organization of U.S. society.

Divisions in the U.S. are not between black and white, citizen and non-citizen, young and old, or gay and straight. The divisions only serve to distract from the development of this new system, which will create new divisions between the educated and uneducated, rich and poor, and have and have nots. When we accept this new understanding of U.S. society, the analysis shifts to relevant issues regarding the value of labour and life. Through this process, all groups can participate in the new discussions of technology and its impact on life, so each person can truly continue to pursue their happiness in this new reality.

The protection of life has to be removed from its connection with labour if it is going to continue to have value in the U.S. system. With scarcity of resources, all groups in the U.S. are grappling with reality in different ways; without a real understanding of their reality, educationally marginalized groups are left farther and farther behind. Careers, jobs, and positions of the past are no longer relevant in the capitalist order that finds the most efficient and cost-effective method to create profit. Older principles of engagement regarding workers will no longer apply. Their disappearance will leave many in the U.S. with less opportunities than their parents.

These outcomes imperil the so-called *American Dream* where each new generation seeks to provide greater advantages for their children. The inability of workers to secure a better future for their children has the potential to undo U.S. capitalism. The development of more efficient and advanced artificial intelligence, robotics, and mechanizations systems continues to globalize labour. So to do they globalize the political, economic, and cultural conversations, as they develop in the U.S. and a pressing question is who must we address these changes in the organization, uses, and value of labour and life in the U.S.

ERICA L. BUMPERS

13. A TALE OF TWO CITIES

A Divide of White and Black Non-Unification

St. Louis, Missouri is located along the Mississippi River. With a circumference of 62 miles, its geographic position and historic ties to the institution of slavery place it on a border between North and South. The Missouri Compromise of 1820 set a precedent in how St. Louis operated in this unique space between slavery and freedom, which can be seen reflected in its relationship with the African American community in twenty-first century.

Ferguson, an area adjacent to St. Louis, is an area where a police officer killed unarmed Michael Brown in the middle of an African American neighbourhood. The events in Ferguson brought about change that energized communities across the world, uniting African Americans and some Whites. At the same time the events divided the nation by exposing a huge disconnect within a predominantly African American neighbourhood run by a predominantly White police department. The news coverage failed, in large order, to explore and examine the fault lines of class, race, and education that remain in the St. Louis area.

Many people question how a predominantly white police department can run a predominantly black neighbourhood. This question has been the topic of many discussions because this has been the history of St. Louis – characterized by a black and white divide throughout the metropolitan area from schools to businesses and housing. The fact remains that class and race impact the demographics of most urban centres, including St. Louis. The centrality of Black and White divisions in St. Louis are problematic, with no real solution.

Some African Americans in St. Louis have been denied the opportunity to develop skills necessary to become productive citizens in society. The systemic inequality that impacts all areas of life in St. Louis. The circumstances have left many people in the most economically exposed areas without the tools they need to compete in the American economy.

As the qualifications of society have become more demanding, the lack of a college degree, ability to participate fully in the economy and contribute to the larger community continues to hamper the development of the African American community. Some argue that African Americans are not productive citizens because they lack these skills. These attitudes present a daunting challenge for many people who reside in St. Louis.

Although the city is known for its Gateway Arch, Dred Scott, Tina Turner, Maya Angelou, Dick Gregory, Nelly, among many others have risen from devastating

© KONINKLIJKE BRILL NV, LEIDEN, 2018 | DOI 10.1163/9789004378735_013

circumstances to become legends. Being one of the largest metropolitan areas of the Midwest, St. Louis has remained segregated from its establishment. Many people migrated to St. Louis in search of a better life to escape the grinding poverty of sharecropping, humiliating injustice of inequality, and blinding racism of the South, but St. Louis still has failed to offer protection from the continuation of these beliefs and practices.

From the reversal of white flight to downtown gentrification, the renewal of this city, beset by racial and class divisions, continue to impact neighbourhood organization, local school choice, and cross-cultural socialization. Some would assume this city thrives on its businesses, economic development, and wealth. However, St. Louis has produced divided action and disharmony within the racial and class boundaries that separate black and white and the rich and poor.

The Delmar Divide, consisting of Delmar Boulevard running East-West, borders the North and South. Delmar demonstrates how St. Louis is divided both from a racial perspective and also from the economic perspective of the haves and have nots. The southern border of Delmar has a predominantly white population with a higher socioeconomic status with homes ranging in value from $300,000 to over $1 million. Welcoming neighbourhoods, manicured lawns, boutiques, antique stores, restaurants, and parks dot the landscape of this upscale area.

Delmar to the north is quite opposite. The southern border is comprised of a predominantly African American population of lower socioeconomic status. Dilapidated neighbourhoods, dilapidated houses, liquor stores on almost every corner, abandoned buildings, and neglected playgrounds line the street. This side of Delmar mirrors other desolate communities located around the country that are considered oppressed and in despair.

The history of Delmar to the south includes a period when it was predominately white with very few African Americans. White flight impacted the area. As African Americans moved into the area, whites started to relocate to the suburbs, leaving this area as a predominately African American neighbourhood.

The Delmar Divide represents a city that continues to segregate racially and socially. It demonstrates how St. Louis has effectively become two cities. The street exemplifies the huge disconnect that exists between the disadvantaged and advantaged, which is and impacted by both wealth and race. Although a racial divide is clearly evident in St. Louis, it cannot move forward due to and become a progressive city. The divide located at Delmar Boulevard that continues to dictate that St. Louis remain a reactionary city.

After the *Brown vs. Board*, St. Louis schools remained segregated. The creation of neighbourhood schools and zoning districts, and subsequent white flight, created a de-facto segregated educational system. Traditionally, Blacks were required to attend schools in their neighbourhoods because there was no mandated rule for the integration of Blacks and Whites. St. Louis was divided into St. Louis City and St. Louis County to separate whites and blacks from attending the same schools.

City schools compared to county schools have many differences in student populations, educational outcomes, and expenditures. St. Louis County schools are considered to be superior to St. Louis City Schools. Years ago, parents of students attending predominately African American St. Louis City Schools argued that their children were receiving an inferior education compared to the predominately white St. Louis County Schools.

This shift created a huge debate and court case. As a result of litigation, a law was passed for students to be bused to St. Louis County schools causing disruption in the St. Louis County schools. The unofficial purpose of the divide of St. Louis County and St. Louis City was to maintain the Black and White spaces, and ensure a distinction between city and county.

The divide of Blacks and Whites continues in St. Louis; it is more visible because of the socioeconomic factors that impact school separation between black and white. Although St. Louis is divided between city and county, the segregation and economics continue to play a major role in the education a person receives, and reinforces how people in St. Louis distinguish educational outcomes and socioeconomic positions.

The common question St. Louis citizens often begin a conversation with is "where did you attend high school?" This seemingly-benign question contributes to a deepening divide that mirrors segregation within the city, precluding any real, effective, and response to the endemic discrimination, educational disadvantages, and economic inequality. Some assume this question is a conversation starter, but often times, it is an attempt to determine the socioeconomic, social, and educational status of the other person. A very disparaging question based on a response is based on the assumption that school attended determines educational outcome and socioeconomic position in society.

The question actually demonstrates how a divided city grounded in a theory of inequality continues to reinforce a stereotype that places people in difficult situations with fewer opportunities for advancement. This theory is influenced by social and cultural factors and the circumstances beyond an individual's control. From the perspective of a native St. Louisan, this question defines an individual's status quo and the divide of St. Louis, eroding all the possibility of a collective action, response, and responsibility to address the political and educational concerns that continue to bifurcate the community.

St. Louis has historically been a metropolitan area divided by class, race, and education. It is divided into black and white, city and county, and socioeconomic status. These factors contribute to the division that exists and why St. Louis is, and continues to remain, segregated. Can St. Louis become a progressive and prosperous city, not by ignoring these problems, but by acknowledging them and trying to solve them?

While the division of Black and White in St. Louis is immediately apparent, the divide of Black and Black is perhaps even more prevalent. The division of Black and Black has caused separation within the city as recently as the city elections of 2017. The mayoral debate consisted of five strong candidates, each with a different platform to transform St. Louis into a city that would never be forgotten. Four of the five candidates were African American, including one woman and a white candidate.

Due to the large number of African American candidates, the Black vote was divided amongst the four candidates. If the African American candidates had come together, they could have presented a united front rather than a division. Coming together would have brought a different perspective to St. Louis, whose mayor has been white for many years. Residents want St. Louis to be a progressive and equitable city, and bring about a change for the better that gives African Americans a voice. St. Louis had the opportunity to make history; it could have elected the first African American woman for office, but the white candidate won the mayoral race by a mere 880 votes.

It is evident that St. Louis has a long way toward unifying white and black divisions that exist, and they are not alone. The mindset of people throughout the United States must change in order to move forward. Protests are beginning to unite African Americans and whites across cities to address the racial divide that prevents any real cross-cultural and multi-racial dialogue from directly impacting the issues U.S. cities face. A new dialectic must involve class, race, and education to move toward a progressive city built on mutual understanding, cooperation, and involvement that can withstand challenges that were evident during the Ferguson crisis.

JAQUIAL DURHAM

14. LIVING IN A WARZONE

As Hurricane Katrina tore through New Orleans and the Gulf Coast, hundreds of thousands were left behind to suffer the ravages of destruction, disease and even death. The majority of these people were poor; nearly all were Black. The federal government's slow response to local appeals for help is, by now, notorious. Despite the cries of outrage that mounted since the levees broke, we have failed to confront the disaster's lesson: to be poor, or black, in today's consumerist society is to be left behind and living in a warzone.

The year was 2005. My big brown eyes gazed at the television set, my small body stretched across the couch with my head on my grandmother's lap, as we watched the national news. I saw so many African people suffering from this tragedy in New Orleans. The natural disaster of Hurricane Katrina was followed by a grossly unnatural government response that killed thousands of vulnerable citizens and co-signed many more to refugee status. There were men and women wading chest-deep in water. If when they weren't floating, they were drowning in the toxic whirlpool the streets of New Orleans had become.

When the water subsided, dead bodies were strewn on curb sides. Others were wrapped in blankets by fellow sufferers, who provided the perished their only dignity. There were thousands of people silently dying from hunger or thirst, writhing in pain, quickly collapsing from missed medications that regulate diabetes, high blood pressure, or cardiac illness.

Though young, I could still see that there was a tremendous shortcoming in the way the government responded to the atrocities in New Orleans. The devastation rendered in New Orleans by Hurricane Katrina took place many years before I realized my passion for political science and advocacy. Yet, still, in my mind, I wanted to know what people could do to help my brothers and sisters who were living in a warzone.

What does it mean to live in a warzone? To live in a warzone means to be vulnerable. In the most basic sense, all of us are vulnerable: to be human is to be susceptible to misfortune, violence, illness, and death. The role of the government, however, is to offer various forms of protection that enhance our lives and shield our bodies from foreseeable and preventable dangers.

To live in a warzone means to be subject to state violence. In recent years, thousands in the U.S. have died at the hands of law enforcement, a reality made even more shameful when we consider how many of these victims were young, poor, mentally ill, Black, and unarmed. To live in a warzone is to be considered disposable.

In Flint, Michigan, we witnessed this century's most profound illustration of civic evil. An entire city was collectively punished with lead-poisoned water for the crime of being poor, Black and politically disempowered. Living in warzone is not having access to fundamental human rights. These rights can be defined as the freedom of movement and expression, freedom to love candidly, freedom to dream, open avenues to advance ourselves through education, equal access to food, clothing, shelter and other basic provisions of life.

WHAT IT MEANS TO LIVE IN A WARZONE

I grew up in a small city in Clemson, South Carolina. Segregated schooling, segregated living and lack of attention to the poor, particularly Black people, was something that often went unspoken. In the culturally traditional South, growing up in a small town meant living in an underemployed and underdeveloped working-class neighbourhood for most people of colour.

As for me, it was a community and culture in which friends and family all too often had one of two paths in life: death or prison. People, particularly Black people, lacked equal access to quality education and had minimal access to jobs that paid liveable wages. As I got older I became more knowledgeable about the dire situation in my community. I realized that my people were living in a warzone all their own. The lack of basic human fundamentals such as education and opportunities for youth mimicked a battlefield for the war waged against people of colour by their own government.

I started to notice these discrepancies in ninth grade. Though white, the school I attended was poor, and most of the parents were working class. The school had, however, basic resources and books. When I was in ninth and tenth grades I attended an alternative school. There I realized key differences between the predominantly white institution I had previously attended and the majority-Black alternative school I was now enrolled in.

The Black school lacked basic resources, including books. When I boarded the bus, I would see my peers from my old school with their books. At the time, it didn't stand out to me that they had books and we did not. This was simply life as I understood it and I had no profound insight into what was going on. However, I most definitely could tell that my old school (which was mainly white, be peppered with a few brown faces) felt significantly different than this alternative institution, which was not a white space.

On September 17th, 2014, Lester "Vari" Mosley Jr. was found guilty of first-degree murder of a 23-year old Clemson University student; Mosely Jr. was sentenced to 50 years in prison. Lester, only 20 years old was a native of Clemson and attended that alternative school with me. Long before Lester Mosley Jr. lost his life to a prison sentence he was a victim of broken schools and abandoned by the state and living in a warzone.

While in Clemson, South Carolina the local government established curfews and tougher laws, those measures were simply band-aids to a deeper problem. In South Carolina, there are schools that are underfunded and unable provide adequate education because of misappropriation of proper resources. Out-of-school and after school resources are unavailable to parents working two to three jobs and physically incapable of being present at all times.

In addition, there is a criminal injustice system that is committed to incarcerating, rather than investing in, young people. Not only was Lester one of the Black students who attended the previously mentioned alternative school, where the quality of education was low, but he also he also fell victim to fundamental inequalities outside of school. Mosley, Jr. was already living in a warzone where he was failed by the state and ultimately the school districts that existed within them.

To be incarcerated was the last stage of the long process that is living in a warzone. I refuse to believe Lester was a criminal or prone to criminality, or even a bad person. The mass incarceration of Black people, males in particular, lends credence to the idea that our criminal justice system that is designed to produced that type of outcome.

The U.S. has seen generations of repetitive incarceration for murder, drug dealing, or drug possession. We should not question of why this is happening, but rather why this is a repetitive cycle. We need to uncover the solutions to end the types of acts that keep Blacks in Clemson from reaching new heights.

Although these issues plague South Carolinians, they are present all across the nation. The U.S. has invested minimum in education, while focusing more on building prisons and jails. The U.S. has literally replaced the language of investment and love with one of containment and blame.

Education is a solution to the large number of African Americans adolescent males as well as adult males who are confined. We live in a nation that is committed to first-class jails and second-class schools. Unfortunately, until the U.S. government can decide that education should be considered a priority and focus on bettering the education of youth, there will be more mass incarcerations and warzones.

A growing number of non-profit organizations in the Clemson area, such as Tempo Sports Academy, have committed to sponsoring Clemson youth with a wide range of services, most notably with academics and athletic growth through mentorship. Lester Mosley, Jr. was a young adult and vulnerable, in a box with a whole class of people, growing in size, desperate in circumstances, living on the edge, living in a warzone.

CONCLUSION

In this chapter I have compared the catastrophe of a warzone to the devastation rampant in poor, Black communities in this country. By spotlighting the fires of social, cultural, and economic conditions that undermine the lives of the vulnerable, I hope to have offered a thicker analysis of the current crisis. At every moment in history, oppression has been met with resistance. In doing so, resisters offer hope that another world is possible, that empires eventually fall, and that freedom is closer than we think.

The solution I would offer as a response to these form of injustices is the process of deep listening. What does it mean to engage in the process of deep listening? Deep listening does not mean that we engage in conversation and wait for our turn to speak. Deep listening means utilizing our voices as citizens of the U.S. in order to force America to amend its broken promises. At this moment, we must not only command the U.S. to listen to new perspectives or old perspectives, but listen to itself and its own democratic promise.

On August 28th, 1963, Martin Luther King, Jr. gave his speech in Washington, D.C. in front of the statue of Abraham Lincoln. Martin Luther King, Jr. told the citizens of the U.S. that "the founding fathers and who symbolic shadows, we stand, signed the emancipation proclamation." What Martin Luther King, Jr. was essentially saying is that the U.S. has made a promise. What we must come to understand is that August 28th, 1963 was not about dreams, instead it was about promises.

America must be forced to listen to its promise. The promises of the Emancipation proclamation, Brown v. Board of Education, and Voting Rights Act, as examples. We must imagine how different the immigration debates would be if we forced the U.S. to listen to its promise of the 14th Amendment or imagine how difficult it would be to engage in mass incarceration if we respected the 6th and 8th Amendment.

We must force the U.S. to not only listen to utterances, new challenges, or to just new ethnics. We must also force the U.S. to listen deeply to its own founding documents. We must want to live in a nation that lives up to its promises and a nation that is as good as its promises.

ANTONIO L. ELLIS AND EDDIE VANDERHORST

15. POLICE BRUTALITY IN NORTH CHARLESTON, SOUTH CAROLINA

Somebody Has to Say Something

As natives of Charleston, South Carolina, we frequent the city of North Charleston, approximately five miles from the inner city of downtown Charleston. Our aim here is to shed light on our experiences with police brutality and racial profiling from North Charleston Police Officers. We also synthesize the voices of local citizens by sharing overarching concerns which erode trust between local citizens and law enforcement. While police brutality is often associated with physical abuse, we challenge readers to think about police brutality also as mental abuse provoked by public shaming and humiliation.

ANTONIO L. ELLIS PROFILED BY NORTH CHARLESTON POLICE OFFICERS

During the fall of 2014, I was driving home after a long day of teaching and grading papers at the College of Charleston. I was abruptly pulled over by a North Charleston police officer. While driving under the speed limit, I vividly recall having seen a Crown Victoria police car following me for approximately three miles.

As I changed lanes, the officer changed lanes while continuing to get closer to the tail end of my car. I concluded that I was being followed, and my heart started racing with anxiety. I immediately thought about the many African American males who were unjustly killed by the state via police brutality. I continued driving nervously, and the officer eventually turned on his blue lights. I pulled over into the margins of the road, stopping in a lighted area to lessen the chances of being physically harmed by the officer.

As I sat waiting on the officer to approach my car, I kept both hands on the steering wheel, while trying to think of additional ways to make the police officer not feel threatened by me. As an African American male who is speech impaired, I was afraid and extremely uncomfortable. At least three minutes passed before the officer finally approached my car and asked for my driver's license and registration.

While the officer was taking my credentials back to his car, I heard police siren sounds approaching from afar off. The sounds continued to get closer by the minute. Eventually I realized the officer who pulled me over had called for backup support. In that moment, my heart started racing and my eyes filled with tears. Seconds later,

© KONINKLIJKE BRILL NV, LEIDEN, 2018 | DOI 10.1163/9789004378735_015

the backup officers aggressively commanded that I step out of my car, place both hands on the hood of my car, and spread my legs. Both officers patted me down and emptied my pockets.

Thereafter, they searched my car. While searching my car, they saw my college faculty identification card under the armrest. One officer asked me if it was a fake faculty identification card. I told him that it was real and that he could look me up on the college website.

At that point, all the officers walked a few feet away and got into a huddle, leaving me with my hands still on the hood and legs spread apart. After approximately five minutes, the officers walked back over to me saying, "you may get back in your car. We looked on the college website to make sure that your faculty identification card was legitimate." When I asked why I was pulled over, one officer said "we thought you were someone else, and you'd better get going."

To avoid further conflicts, I left the scene with anger in my heart. I felt as if I was initially stereotyped and profiled as a Black male driving through the city of North Charleston; and yet somewhat privileged once the officers realized my professional status as a faculty member at a popular local predominantly white college.

EDDIE VANDERHORST PROFILED BY NORTH CHARLESTON POLICE OFFICERS

It was a cold wintery night in 2006, when I was driving through North Charleston with my two-year-old daughter in the back seat. As I was traveling through the city, I became alarmed as blue lights and sirens came on behind me. Not only was I alarmed, my two-year-old daughter was even more alarmed, as she began to cry and scream hysterically at a very loud volume.

In the moment, I tried to calm her down, while concurrently trying to figure out why I was being pulled over by the police. When the officer approached my car, he shone his flashlight into my daughter's face and demanded that I do something to "shut the baby up." At that point, I became furious internally with the police for using such language while referencing my daughter. My first thought was "who in the hell is he talking to?" but, I did not allow my anger and inner rage to cause me to act out of character in front of my daughter.

Thereafter, the officer asked me for the license and registration. When he went back to his car with my credentials, I used that time to calm my daughter's emotions to the best of my ability. Nevertheless, she was physically shaking and breathing heavily at an abnormally fast pace.

While I was feared for my safety, my primary concern was the comfort of my daughter. In the midst of my comforting my daughter, as in the previous testimony, more police cars arrived on the scene. I was told to step out of my car, while leaving my daughter in the car alone. When my daughter noticed that I was exiting the car, she became even more emotional than she had been initially.

As I carefully exited the car, two officers abruptly pushed me against my car and proceeded to handcuff me. Although I was being physically abused by the police officers, I still was focused on the well-being of my daughter. As the officers were using excessive force on me, I asked if they could call one of my family members to come and get my daughter.

One officer called the number I provided, while the other informed me that I was being detained due to my suspended driver's license. While driving with a suspended license might warrant an arrest, it does not justify the fact that I was physically abused by the officers. I did not resist arrest, nor did I pose a threat to them. In addition, my two-year-old daughter should not have been traumatized by professionals who are hired to protect citizens. I often wonder if I would have been treated differently if I was a professor at a prestigious local college, like my co-author.

LOCAL CITIZENS' PERCEPTION OF NORTH CHARLESTON POLICE OFFICERS

Local citizens in the city of North Charleston are constantly fearful that their lives will be unjustly taken by a police officer. While the shooting of Walter Scott brought national attention to police brutality in North Charleston, the unjust treatment of citizens in the city is nothing new to the local residents. The dichotomized perspective of law enforcement in North Charleston is built upon a history of distrust. We assert that there has not been trust between local citizens within urban communities and police officers as long as we remember. There is an overarching belief that is embedded within the consciousness of Black residents of North Charleston.

Those who reside in these communities believe that local police officers use Black, poor, and vulnerable people to prosper economically. For example, it's widely believed that North Charleston police officers target Black males at night and plant illegal drugs on them. Many also believe that the same police officers give local citizens speeding tickets illegally in order to make their quarterly quota. In addition, we have overheard fellow community members mention the fact that local police officers handcuff Black males, while taking their money for personal use during the search and seizure process; however, in many such instances, they do not make an arrest.

Even given these examples of police misconduct, police support still appears to be strong among citizens who live in the suburbs of North Charleston, while citizens who reside in urban centers lack trust due to their personal experiences. Instead of local citizens viewing police officers as professionals who will protect them, they see police as people who sabotage and physically harm Black bodies with no remorse. In some cases, police officers in North Charleston have been known to mentally abuse and publicly shame citizens, as they did with Antonio earlier in this chapter.

As fear continues to penetrate the hearts and minds of local citizens, it is imperative that community organizers hold local elected officials accountable for challenging unethical behaviors of law enforcement. Over the last three years, local civil rights leaders in North Charleston have hosted marches and rallies to draw attention to police brutality in light of the murder of Walter Scott. While marches and rallies are somewhat useful, marching and rallying alone does not create systemic change.

We contend that change is more likely to occur when local officials are provoked to make public policy decisions regarding law enforcement, which would in turn hold police officers accountable. To this extent, we believe that a local Civilian Review Board (CRB) should be formed in the city of North Charleston. The primary purpose of a CRB is to ensure that police are complying with local and federal laws, in addition to facing the necessary consequences when they fail to comply with the law.

CONCLUSION

African Americans and other minority groups have experienced social, economic, and political progress in America. Beyond those struggles, the treatment of people of colour by law enforcement remains a national dilemma in the city of North Charleston and throughout the U.S. African Americans, unfortunately, are seemingly targeted more than any other minority group.

It is imperative that we remain sober-minded, engage in protests, and ensure that our local elected officials are visible and vocal in regard to the safety of the beloved community. While not every assault on communities of colour may be publicized nationally like the Walter Scott case, we encourage local citizens to remain dedicated to ensuring that our government demand law enforcement follow the same laws that they enforce. Unfortunately, based on our experiences, we contend that most minorities in North Charleston live in fear because the professionals who are sworn in to protect citizens so commonly betray them.

Not only must we depend on our local elected officials to speak truth to power, we implore citizens to ensure that social justice and faith-based organizations are active participants in the continued pursuit of equity. If law enforcement officers continue to invoke fear in our communities, we doubt that trust can ever be built. While we continue to fight for justice we must remain vigilant by striving to ensure that all citizens are safe.

As African American men, one a professor of education and another an aspiring professor of criminology, we are constantly thinking about ways to ensure that Black lives will one day matter to all law enforcement throughout the United States of America. While we centered our discussion on police brutality in North Charleston, South Carolina, we advocate for equity and fairness broadly.

DELEON M. WILSON

16. AN INSPIRED PROTEST

Notes from Baton Rouge 2016 Protests

June 8–14, 2016 – He is so small and precious, perfect in every way. My brother picks up my second nephew and says, "Here, godmother, get to know your godchild," and a baby appears in my arms. Looking at him, I remember feeling every emotion of joy and love possible. I make myself an inner promise to always do everything in the world to love, protect, and make a better world for him and his older brother, both Black boys (the youngest biracial) born into a very imperfect world.

July 5, 2016 – There is a story and video of a man, brutally shot by police, on Facebook. While I can no longer be surprised by this level of violence, I am once more dismayed that it happened to another Black man, who is seemingly unarmed. He's big guy, like so many other kind Black men I know. There's nothing scary about him. He's dark skinned with gold teeth in the front of his mouth. In his picture, he is smiling. The man's name was Alton Sterling. The outrage on my Facebook is great, and then I realize, this happened in Baton Rouge. It was only a matter of time.

July 6, 2016 – A second video emerges. It is really hard to watch. I wish I hadn't. I watch the life leave from this man's body as a police officer held a gun to his chest, while on top of him. The police say he was reaching for a gun, but I see both hands restrained in the footage. The news plays the footage, blurred because of bloodshed in the video. They just left him lying there, dying. I keep replaying the image of his life leaving his body in my head. I feel sick, mentally and physically sick.

July 7, 2016 – My boyfriend leaves with a group of friends, all Black, on a bachelor party trip for his best friend. I feel exceptionally worried. I keep my thoughts to myself. I wonder what a group of young Black men are going to encounter on the road to Texas. The Baton Rouge Police Department is horribly on edge, only traveling in packs. The group left early Thursday morning for Texas, not to return until Sunday. I stay in bed the entire day, nervous and nauseous. Nothing seems safe or innocuous for Black males anymore.

July 9, 2016 – My friend calls me to relay that she and her future sister-in-law are going to a protest downtown. She is not letting me stay in bed all day. I am not quite sure if I want to join; then I remember the tearful woman on the news, Alton's aunt, who raised him. If something were to happen to my nephews, I would be destroyed. I look at the picture of my nephews I saved as my lock screen wallpaper. I see their sweet faces, so young and unknowing of the ugliness of this world. They cannot fight for themselves, so Aunt De/Maran has to for them. "I'm in," I reply.

© KONINKLIJKE BRILL NV, LEIDEN, 2018 | DOI 10.1163/9789004378735_016

I call my mother and let her know I am going to a protest downtown. She sits silent, then gives me a dry "okay," her way of letting me know she disapproves. I can tell she is worried for my safety. Being a child of segregation, she knows very well the dangers of protesting.

The protest is peaceful. Only one food establishment is open; the rest are closed for fear of rioting. There has always been an unnecessary fear of Black people in Baton Rouge, so I guess protests are making the locals even more nervous.

We head to ground zero of the next protest, across the street from the main headquarters of the Baton Rouge Police Department. The protesters are gathered at the Circle K across the street. One woman loudly yells at the crowd to band arms across Airline Highway. She yells her message proudly, asking the crowd not to fear repercussions, and is promptly taken down and arrested by several large police officers. She probably weighs 100 pounds soaking wet. The police move to "control" the crowd, lining up in the middle of Airline Highway opposite the protestors. The police are arresting anyone who stands or places a foot onto the road, and yet, they march and gather in the middle of the road, stopping traffic to set up for a crowd dispersal. My friends are in the front of the crowd, but I remain in the back, listening to people talk about the current events.

"These police are fucking crazy!"

"Why the hell did they call Livingston Parish sheriff here. They know all them motherfuckas are racists!"

"These niggas here are some serious bitches. Why they bringing tanks, here? Ain't nobody got guns!"

As I look around, it becomes clear that people from many backgrounds are gathered to exercise their right to protest and peaceful assembly. I am a part of something bigger than myself.

While the police officers stand in line in the road, I join a conversation with the manager of the Circle K. The store is closed, but there is bottled water outside for anyone to drink. The manager tells me the store voluntarily offered water to the protestors, and how during the day, the protest remained peaceful. She shares her disappointment that the media never showed the protest during the day, which involved families with signs, picnicking with their children. Later in the year, a police officer will say that the protestors were looting water from the Circle K the night of the protest; that will be reported on the news. The media never checks their sources.

Like a call to battle, the police begin to beat their batons on their shields, CLACK, CLACK, CLACK, CLACK! They shout out orders to each other. The crowd begins to chant louder, "no justice no peace, no racist police." I join in enthusiastically. Most of the police force in front of me are white and stone-faced, but one officer stood out.

Black, young, and visibly shaking, I swear I see him crying, though I could not differentiate between sweat and tears. What I see is later confirmed by my friend.

I am taken aback for a moment, realizing the protest was for him, too. I can imagine how much grief Black people give him for being a cop, and how much hardship others give him when he is not wearing that uniform.

The protest becomes heated when the police begin arresting people in the crowd, some innocent bystanders who were accidentally pushed into the roadway. I spot a student from my school being confronted by a police officer. I advance toward him. She escapes into the crowd running from the curb of the road. She is rather emotional, cursing and screaming, but unharmed. Another young man is tackled by the gas pumps, beaten with a club, and arrested. The areas by the gas pumps are supposed to be areas where you can safely stand and observe the protest, yet police officers are advancing on this area as well.

Children around me run frantically to get out of the way. Once several arrests are made, the police retreat back to the roadway. The local news media cameras begin to shine, but only when police are not arresting or physically harming protestors. I hear the report, full of bias and lies. I hear the outrage around me. "Bitch, why are you lying to that camera?" someone shouts. The media tells nothing of what is actually taking place. Meanwhile, national news media take care to interview protestors and tape any violence.

My friends and I evade police advances a few more times during the night. Others around us are not as lucky. A large group of protesters marches toward the interstate to block it; they are brutally subdued. I meet the young woman who organized the protest for that night. I commend her for gathering Black people around a cause in Baton Rouge. I smirk at the sight of winded police officers, sweating, eyes full of hatred. Mentally, I commend them too, because even if it was only for a little while, they helped Black folks in the city gather around a cause and get along, too.

Later in the evening, I receive a phone call from my mom. My brother was on the line with her, and he was more than upset with me. My brother lets it be known he is not happy that I was protesting. I explain to him that I was aiming at more than acceptance from my friends. I had to do it for my students and all young Black people who are misunderstood on a regular basis. How long are Black people supposed accept the status quo, when it is severely unfair?

What happens if injustice continues to happen to those who look like us? I explain to my brother that I was out there fighting for my nephews because one day, they too, would be Black boys and men. I would not know what to do if something like this happened to them. My brother replies sternly, "really? So what am I going to tell them if they lose their aunt and godmother? How do I explain that to them? What do you think that will do to them if they lose you?" I sit in silence. I have no recourse.

July 10, 2016 – I drive to downtown Baton Rouge to join another protest, lead by local youth in the community. It is peaceful, but I miss most of it. While I was driving, I had noticed a large number of military tactical vehicles emblazoned with the name of the local police force on the doors. I had known something was wrong. I immediately text my friends to leave downtown, knowing trouble is on the way. Another protest has broken out downtown, this time more police violence being enacted on white people. It too made the news, but the truth rang supreme on social media.

July 17, 2016 – I am returning to Louisiana from a trip to Austin, Texas. My phone erupts with alerts from my local media apps. Several officers have been shot on this Sunday morning in Baton Rouge, and three have died. More blood has been shed because the of the faulty decision-making of another. Today's shooting was done by a man from out of town who wanted vengeance on the local police force, to make a statement. Protests are halted from this day forth.

***

I have no regrets about protesting; in fact, I feel more empowered. The students who saw me out there with them, gathered for a cause, see me and have a different level of respect, as I respect them. For once, I unabashedly stand for something. Does protesting work? I'm not sure. It didn't stop locals from saying, "I wish they would block roads where I'm living. I'd run all those niggers over," expressing no regard for the children who were there, too. Why is it that Black people and children still have no humanity in the eyes of so many of my neighbours? Sure, "… not all white people …" but many of them.

Systems of power are at play, as there were last summer. It is our responsibility to identify and resist these systems, even when they do not target us in a moment. By day I dedicate my time to teaching children how to find their own truths, so the media does not dictate their minds and actions. I understood my responsibility that summer. Protesting gave me an unedited view into the world around me. Writing articles from my safe place and watching hours of news stories could never offer me this view. I fight and I protest because there will always be two young, brown faces looking at me on my phone's lock screen, pushing me to do and be more.

TAHAREE A. JACKSON

17. WE DON'T WANT NO TROUBLE

Inspiring White Accomplices and Solidarity in the Age of All Lives Matter

As a multiracial daughter of the South, I have experienced how Black people routinely avoid police harassment, arrest, and death with these simple words: "We don't want no trouble." Throughout enslavement, Jim Crow, and even now, we use this phrase to indicate our immediate surrender when we interface with law enforcement, authorities of any kind, or White people who are uncomfortable in our presence. Whites also use this as a polite way to warn minorities of ensuing calls to the police if we do not remove ourselves from an unwelcome space.

THE REAL TROUBLEMAKERS: THEN AND NOW

Despite our storied mix, my brother is a dark-skinned Black man. A locomotive engineer and avid beer drinker, he tries to enjoy bars that dot his rail route along the southern seaboard. He regularly enters a watering hole, quietly joins a crowd, orders a beer, and is quickly told, "Tab? We don't want no trouble." He pays for a few sips and leaves. His sister teaches a diversity course to 30 future educators, none of whom are Black. There are mumblings about grades: "Can you believe she questioned my word choice? Which 'grammar' mistakes is she referring to?" She ... I ... stay after class fielding questions from White students who need to "know more" about how I arrived at a 1-point deduction. "We're just asking." Translation: "We don't want no trouble, but there will be if you don't answer."

As sister to a Black man and long-time teacher educator, I find it increasingly necessary to move White people from actors to allies to accomplices in the struggle for racial justice. If we are to make optimal progress in avoiding the trauma, pain, and death caused by unmitigated racism, involving White people – dare I say even *focusing* on White people – is crucial. As Blacks are gunned down over assumptions based on their skin, we desperately need solidarity with Whites. We need White people to stir up trouble, but the right kind.

One response to the violence against Black bodies is the Black Lives Matter movement. Despite the problematic nature of "All Lives Matter," and the emboldened resurgence of Trump-inspired, anti-minority sentiment, there is a way forward, restoring Black and Brown communities. From my vantage point it involves dramatic paradigm shifts in White people who tout not "wanting any trouble," yet actively

© KONINKLIJKE BRILL NV, LEIDEN, 2018 | DOI 10.1163/9789004378735_017

create and participate in it each day. The complicity is the wrong kind of trouble, bred from xenophobia, the fear of others, and the fragility that ensues when White people feel threatened, minoritized, or disempowered. The trouble requires troubling itself.

ENOUGH ABOUT YOU. LET'S TALK ABOUT ME

I have had little choice in working with White people; nearly 90% of teachers are White. As a professor of courses focused on minority and urban education, it is my job to usher educators from witnesses (actors) of racism, to advocates (allies) against racism. Advocates become "the new troublemakers" (accomplices) who stand in full, disruptive solidarity with people who are racially disenfranchised. In what Johnathan Osler has referred to as the progression from actors to allies to accomplices, my mission of late has been to move novice teachers even further along the spectrum of solidarity in response to increased hate, heightened intolerance, and state-sanctioned vitriol from the schoolhouse to the courthouse to the White House.

The film *Hidden Figures* (2016) contains a telling scene that captures the historic use of the "We don't want no trouble" device to exonerate White people from racial violence and then position them as victims of the very racism they stir up. Programming expert Dorothy Vaughn and her children were quietly perusing books in a public library when a White librarian accosted her about why she was not in the coloured section. When Vaughn bemoaned the absence of what she needed, the librarian responded, "Well that's just the way it is. We don't want any trouble."

The Black woman and her children were then thrown out, and a White police officer violently assisted. This was never about the presence of a Black woman and her well-behaved children causing trouble. Rather, "trouble" itself was brewed up and escalated into spectacle based on the discomfort of a White woman and her bystanding actors. Complicit in her racism, White patrons watched as a Black family was dragged out in an undignified fashion.

Troublingly ironic about this scene (and every other time Whites deploy a false claim of "not wanting any trouble" but simultaneously create racial uproar) is that I continue to observe modern instantiations of this behaviour. This scene plays out in my brother's bars, in my mostly White classes, and in nightly newscasts where Whites are outraged by the disruptions caused by Black Lives Matter protests, but undisturbed by the rampant racism that caused whichever Black death *prior to* the protests. We can fill these blanks with Trayvon Martin, Sandra Bland, and the many other Black lives lost without their demise captured on film.

As a teacher educator of predominantly White students, I am met with repeated resistance to discussions of racism, not the least of which is dedication to the All Lives Matter "movement." This, along with Blue Lives Matter, is a sorry attempt to decenter state-sponsored violence against minorities by equating the loss of police officers themselves or any other life, for any reason other than racism.

These "All Lives Matter" responses are deeply problematic for their refusal to acknowledge the actual, well-documented, disproportionate loss of innocent Black lives at the hands of law enforcement. As curriculum theorist Michael Apple said, this is a maneuver of Whites who are essentially saying, "Enough about you. Let's talk about me."

I posit that by critically focusing on whiteness, we can successfully include White people in conversations about race by redirecting attention to their responsibilities for quelling racism in and among themselves. Malcom X and many others have argued that the most sorely needed racial work need not occur with Blacks and populations besieged by racial violence, but by those who manufacture and perpetuate it – White people.

SOLIDARITY IN THE STREETS AND IN THE SHEETS

As a professor, I study how people in privileged groups become advocates and allies for "others." How do wealthy people like Warren Buffet become anti-classist and rally *against* tax cuts for the rich? How do men become feminist and fight domestic violence and rape culture, and then march alongside women across the nation? And how do White people, who undeniably benefit from systemic racism, come to denounce white privilege and racial supremacy to the point that they protest with Black Lives Matter and risk arrest themselves? How do we get more White people to do that and more?

Ironically, White people's quickness to proclaim that they "don't want no trouble" is a double negative, and I need this to be true. I need White people NOT to want to call the police whenever they feel uncomfortable around us. I need White people NOT to want to exclude us based solely on our skin. I need White people to take this phrase, co-opt it, and mean what they say. What does it mean to move White people from the real troublemakers to makers of the kind of trouble that eradicates racism? Does it involve working closely with People of Color? Does it involve charging us with all the racial work? No. When Malcolm X was asked what sincere White people could do, his reply was clear:

> Where the really sincere white people have got to do their "proving" of themselves is not among the black victims, but out on the battle lines of where America's racism really is – and that's in their own home communities; America's racism is among their own fellow whites. That's where sincere whites who really mean to accomplish something have got to work.

The accomplice framework is compelling because it directly responds to Malcolm X's charge to White people. Actors simply watch as people of colour are hurt or even killed by other white actors. They may feel some sense of guilt or shame, but they don't challenge the situation or institutional racism itself.

Allies stand in solidarity with People of Colour and are motivated by working with them in comfortable, cross-racial settings. *Accomplices,* however, are not motivated by a need to pacify their White guilt or to "salve their consciences," in Malcom's words. These White people have not held on to their "Obama for America" pins as a literal badge of their fidelity to Black people or their implied exoneration from racism. They don't proudly proclaim, "I voted for Obama," and they do not begin sentences with "Not all White people" when you describe widespread racism.

Accomplices are cut from a different cloth. They represent a new ilk of White folk who are not only willing to protest in the streets, but tackle racism in their sheets. These white people stand in full solidarity with People of Color in public ways, but they take on anti-racist work in the most intimate parts of their lives. These White people are fully "woke," and they are ready to sacrifice a friendship, partner, or job to stand on the side of justice. These White people are not evading conversations about race. Rather, they stir up conversations about race and *the right kind of trouble* with the very people who need them the most – their own.

I am convinced that White people have always (and will always be) been necessary in the fight for racial freedom. From abolition to suffrage to queer rights, our best efforts in achieving civil rights in any realm has been cross-racial. We have accomplished the most progress with all hands on deck, with protests in the streets, fierce conversations between the sheets, and with sincere White people understanding their privilege and the dehumanization linked to it. They do not divorce their white superiority from their own suffering; they are determined to dismantle the very system that advantages them in real ways, but ultimately robs them of their selfhood.

As a teacher educator, I will continue to teach the history of racism to a mostly White audience. I will challenge master narratives of "work hard, get what you deserve," and I will demonstrate how the myth of meritocracy is a White-empowering farce that ultimately serves no one. I will continue to teach teachers how to value all perspectives, fully recognizing that there are equally viable ways of living which have *nothing* to do with being White.

I will keep studying woke White accomplices who provide exemplars for other Whites who know something is racially amiss, but do not know how to fight. Most importantly, I will keep being a minority professor in a sea of White scholars because it is just as, if not *more important* for White students to experience the dissonance of learning from a brilliant multiracial professor as it is for my students of colour to see themselves and their counterstories represented in my Brown body.

I will continue to talk about whiteness because my students need a model for how to go home and talk to the people they love. Where I cannot be effective in convincing Whites of the racism, violence, and the trouble we see every day, they can. In Malcolm's words, White people can't teach what they don't know, and they won't lead where they won't go. Well ... they have to go home, don't they? And they have to host dinners with racist family members and guests. I may not be coming to dinner, but my woke White accomplices will be there representing my interests.

My goal in teaching and talking about whiteness is to inspire White accomplices who are looking for trouble. Not the kind that results in the police being summoned and someone dying while Black. These "new White troublemakers" look for trouble in all the right spaces because they look in all the *White* spaces. And because of us, they are ready.

TIFFANY HOLLIS

18. ON THE FRONTLINES

The Role of Social Media in the Charlotte Protests

Police brutality is not a new topic in the United States (U.S.). The recent shootings of young black men by law enforcement officers, however, has caused this issue to be at the forefront of local, national, and even international media outlets. There have been numerous protests and riots owing to a lack of indictments for police officers killing unarmed young black men. And, a new social movement was formed that started out as a hashtag: #BlackLivesMatter.

The civil rights movement is also nothing new to in the U.S. #BLM, as a particular movement, comes at a time when the U.S. sees itself as a *colorblind* or *post-racial* society. In fact, the election of a Black president and an increase in the number of Black millionaires, entertainers, athletes, etc. who have reached new levels of economic, social, and educational success could be interpreted as progress among people of colour.

The killings of Black and Brown men at the hands of the police officers is nothing new. We can go as far back as Emmitt Till and even farther back to the lynchings and unjustified murders of Black males during slavery. Ironically, many of the murderers go free and are not indicted and some are even acquitted of all charges. In many of those cases, there was not any video capturing the footage of these incidents. Consequently, the lack of evidence often played a role in those indictments and acquittals. Unfortunately, eyewitness testimony is often not trusted in the court of law. As a result, the public began to ask for body cameras. But, in some of the cases, there was video and still no indictments.

Trayvon Martin, Tamir, Rice, Eric Gardner – these are all names that the nation remembers. Of course, there are many more names of Black and Brown men and women who were murdered by cops or vigilante gunmen. The city of Charlotte, NC can now add the names of Jonathan Farrell and Keith Lamont Scott to the list of Black men who were killed by officers in what were both categorized as a 'justifiable homicide.'

According to police, officers saw Scott exit a vehicle in the parking lot while carrying a *handgun*. They claimed he refused to comply with their orders. Many of the residents stated that he parked there daily and waited for his son's bus to arrive. Keith Lamont Scott's daughter released a video calling the police murderers. stating that her father had a book and not a gun and that they had shot him in cold blood. She could be heard screaming expletives and crying on the video, which soon went viral. Many people watching her video on Facebook Live eventually came over to the location where the incident had taken place.

Many people were angered and outraged. The truth is, the Keith Lamont Scott shooting sparked waves of activism across Charlotte, as tragedy that once seemed distant, was happening right in our backyards. The Facebook Live feed, the Instagram videos, and the pictures on Twitter provided many with up to date and minute-by-minute updates of the incident that had taken place where an officer had killed yet another Black man. The crowd began to gather just feet away from where Keith Lamont Scott had been murdered by a police officer.

Many of the peaceful protests were being captured on Facebook Live and Instagram; while, others were tweeting and posting pictures on Twitter. The videos of the peaceful protests soon turned into chaos as police showed up with riot gear on and started making demands of the peaceful protesters. When protesters did not respond to the demands shouted out by the police, rubber bullets and tear gas were released into the crowd, causing chaos to erupt as many people began to flee or fight back just feet away from where Scott had been shot just hours before.

A young man covered the tragedy over the next few hours for the entire Facebook world to see. Primed by the highly publicized incident of justice that unfolded following the murder of Trayvon Martin and many other Black men and women over recent years, I tuned into the gruesome event as it unfolded. I shared in the visceral impact that this real-time crisis was having on the young man.

The documentation on Facebook Live served as a crucial component for the forthcoming explosion of protests and actions against racial injustice and police brutality across the nation. Footage from the Facebook Live showed things got a little hectic and police started firing off tear gas and the crowd dispersed only to lock the highway, protesting on the Interstate even burning the contents of a tractor trailer truck in the middle of the interstate. The police were able to disperse the crowds and regain some order of the situation – at least for that night.

Several incidents took place across Charlotte the next day as many of the residents were left trying to make sense of the events that transpired. In fact, over the next few days, a familiar trauma swept across Black America. The trauma has reminded us of the "threat" that unarmed men of colour pose and how the police can frame a story to make it seem as if Black men are dangerous or aggressive.

On September 21, 2016, students at UNC Charlotte organized a die-in at the student union. There were chants, songs, and even messages of solidarity among the over 300 students. The die-in was in response to the murder of the unarmed Black man who had a Traumatic Brain Injury, Keith Lamont Scott.

Several protesters joined the call to protest. This time, they met in downtown Charlotte. People from all over Charlotte and even surrounding counties joined this call and marched through the streets to share in the outrage, actions, and demands of local Charlotte activists on the ground. As the protesters marched down the streets of Charlotte NC, many of them held their hands up in the universal sign of surrender while shouting, "HANDS UP! DON'T SHOOT!

Marching alongside a White man were the tiny feet of a 7-year old Black girl. She held a small "It was a book" sign and chanting with as much vigour as the older Black woman who walked slightly ahead of the young girl. You could hear the chants together as the protesters shouted to the world with every fibre of their beings that if there is NO JUSTICE! there will be NO PEACE! Protesters were met with tear gas, rubber bullets, etc. The events that led up to what happened next will be etched into the memory of many of the people who were in the trenches and on the ground marching and many who were watching the events unfold on Facebook live.

The protests and anger that erupted on the streets of uptown Charlotte were unlike any concerted outburst against racial injustice in America that we had witnessed for decades. Led by young local residents of Charlotte, hours of protests were intentionally sustained and met with military presence. That presence included tanks, machine guns, tear gas, and rubber bullets that were released onto protesters.

Very different accounts of these live events were fed to the general public via mainstream and social media. Mainstream media vilified Scott's character through images a joint that he had smoked and hyper visualized the small pool of protesters who were committing violent acts. Social media told stories of excessive force by officers, of united outrage by the exercising their first amendment right, demanding answers, and of legitimate pain in the face of continuous racism against their community.

Social media feed caused many of the residents to experience the trauma of the riots and protests vicariously. Some youth were actually on the frontlines going Live on Facebook, sending minute-by-minute tweets, and even using trending hashtags to garner support around the issue that they were protesting. Although the media was covering the violence, social media feeds were providing the general public a different perspective of what was taking place.

Calls for peace from various leaders in Charlotte were met with chants as many people realized that it was bigger than a call for peace. The call was for improved relations between the police and the communities they serve. Despite the protests, a clear strategy for more equitable systems of justice, politics, housing, and education does not seem to be on the horizon; despite a lack of a clear strategy, many continue to fight for justice on the front lines.

ERIN DREESZEN

19. TRUTHS WE DON'T SHARE

I don't make tacos for dinner anymore. I was preparing tacos the day tragedy struck my family. I recall all too clearly, my newborn boy bouncing in his chair behind me as his big sister was attempting to write a story at the counter. The beef had just started to sizzle when the phone rang. My father's voice, shaken and distraught, signalled to me that something was not right. He told me to sit down and I immediately asked if my grandpa was okay.

"Yes, punkin, he's fine. Are you sitting down? "

"Daddy, what's wrong?"

"Your beautiful brother ..."

... and with those words the phone crashed across the room. I didn't want to hear what my father was saying, I already knew enough. My brother, a Federal Law Enforcement Officer, Nathan J. Schuldheiss, was due to return from his deployment in Iraq in three weeks. Only three more weeks and we would have been sharing Thanksgiving dinner at our mother's house. Now it was my responsibility to drive across town and tell our mother that our lives would never be the same again. As a result of my personal experience with tragedy, the tragic events between law enforcement and communities of colour have significantly influenced how I perceive truth.

When tragedy strikes, some are overcome with silence and tears while others are consumed with rage and unanswered questions. Regardless of the response, it is human nature to search for answers behind the why in an attempt to gain understanding. Not an understanding of the philosophical meaning of life, or the reason a life might end before it really started, or even how to prevent the occurrence from repeating itself – we want to make sense of something so incomprehensible, something that forever disrupts the normalcy of daily experiences.

Tragedy is an unfortunate event that happens to others, on the news, not to us. We are often unprepared. Out typical human response is to make sense through the lens of fictional divisions of good and bad, innocent and guilty, where roles of heroes and villains are assigned.

There are times when these tragedies are so great they impact a nation. As a nation, a jury of observers, we begin to make sense of tragedies by determining who is innocent and who is guilty. Communities tell their version of a story of justice and blame in the wake of tragedy. It is possible that the tragedies of Trayvon Matrin, Alton Sterling, Philando Castile and Dylan Nobel, and those of Brent Thompson, Patrick Zamarripa, Debra Clayton, or Mark Renniger exposed the narratives of good versus evil in our communities.

Or maybe these events only intensified the disdain that was lurking under the surface due to centuries of racial oppression. In each of these examples the distinctions between good and evil were introduced; ultimately, the distinctions dividing average citizens from our nation's law enforcement officers, those committed to protect and serve.

The International Association of Chiefs of Police requires Law Enforcement Officers take an Oath of Honour as part of their commitment to protect and serve. They promise never to betray their badges and always to uphold their communities. As individuals, their definitions of community could differ, especially when communities are already torn and divided.

A lack of self-awareness and bias often is present in these moments. Project Implicit at Harvard University claims that implicit bias can be masked in two different ways. The first form of implicit bias is an individual's unwillingness to admit truth because it is counter to a person's socially accepted norms. The second form of implicit bias is a lack of awareness that a counter narrative or alternative truth could exist in any given situation. Our fractured lens and unconscious biases set the framework for misinterpretation.

Imagine, for example, you have been working late hours into the night. You are tired and your work has not been especially eventful. Suddenly, from the corner of your eye, you notice something. Your two childhood heroes, the greatest baseball has to offer, are walking down the street toward you. You muster the courage to approach your heroes and ask for a photo. You are shocked that they oblige. A simple selfie request turns into the chance of a lifetime to share in a great conversation about the upcoming season.

Or maybe, you feel the summer heat on your back and you look up, grateful for the trees in the park, your park. Your children are laughing, big smiles and innocent eyes, as they spin faster on the merry-go-round. All the cares and demands of the world fall away as you focus on their eager excitement and desire to take on the challenge of speeding down the slide. Today, it is easy to get lost in the dreams of their future and the adults they will soon become.

These narratives are true experiences of two real people, before tragedy stuck in the summer of 2016. Their race and gender are of no significance. What matters is that they were people who lived and loved and are still loved. They could be anyone enjoying life's simple moments.

Officer Patrick Zamarripa misinterpreted the situation in Dallas after he encountered Nomar Mazara and Joey Gallo of the MLB Texas Rangers. The players later posted their thanks to the fallen Dallas police officer on Twitter stating that he was the true hero in their picture.

Zamarripa and the other officers killed in Dallas will forever be identified by the events of that mournful day when a sniper chose to act on his rage towards white police officers by opening fire. It is an honour to celebrate their full lives before the tragedy and their sacrifice.

Similarly, sitting under the park trees on that hot summer day, Alton Sterling could have never imagined the events that would end his life on July 5, 2016 when two police officer held him down in a convenience store parking lot. The event was captured by onlookers as multiple shots were fired into his chest. Alton Sterling had never met the actress Issa Rae who led numerous members of the Baton Rouge community to establish a scholarship fund in support of his five children, children who should be reminded of the man their father was; supportive, caring, the "CD man" that could strike up a conversation with anyone he met.

Professor Peniel E. Joseph emphasized that those in the U.S. need to confront the pain of black history to embrace the necessary change that would rid the U.S. of racial stigma. Equally important, those in the U.S. need to celebrate experiences of humanity in lives lost. Through stories, where innocent and guilty are humanized, communities can begin to bridge the gap that currently separates them due to historical oppression and current misunderstandings. Americans need to celebrate experiences of humanity, share their truth's, feel as if they can engage in dialogue without humiliation, demonization, vilification or shame.

Engraved in the wall at the National Law Enforcement Officers Memorial in Washington DC are the words *It is not how these officers died that made them heroes, it is how they lived.* All lives matter to those who have been loved and lost through the violence of misunderstanding, misjudgement and mistrust. Yet communities still create these divisions. In the aftermath of those lost in Baton Rouge, Ferguson, and Dallas, several communities created divides between innocence and guilt based on racial differences. These divides allow communities to process the aftermath of a tragedy with one another, but they also limit the experiences and opportunities to learn together.

Instead we rely on news commentary for up-to-date retellings of various versions of events that are easily misunderstood. We impose our implicit and unconscious bias, forming judgments of others we do not know. And finally fear and the desire for accountability develops, preventing us from building the bridges constantly promised by community leaders and politicians. Nothing changes and young black men remain afraid of the truth and potential for ridicule when approached by law enforcement.

My brother, Nathan Schuldheiss, visited villages in Iraq, providing paper and pencils to school children and building relationships with local people. He was attempting to fulfil the promise made by both the American and Iraqi governments, with the intent to change the guilty narrative the Iraqi people have towards Americans. Nathan wanted the next generation of Iraqis to experience Americans as offering goodwill and support.

Instead, there are now ten more families that mourn their own losses, including the families of the men responsible for setting the improvised explosive device that took my brother's life and the lives of two other federal agents. These men were captured, found guilty of their actions and sentenced to their own deaths, executed by firing squad. This accountability did not end the violence in Iraq or give hope for newfound relationships between the Iraqi people and Americans. The legacy and potential for hope that SA Nathan Schuldheiss had intended was lost in continued tragedy, reinforced by untold stories.

We must break the cycle of supposed justice and guilt built upon false pretences of accountability. Not even a week after the death of Alton Sterling, his eldest son, Cameron Sterling, spoke out on CNN about the accountability we all need to have. "My father was a good man ... everyone should be together and not against each other. Everyone needs to be on one accord." He also reminded us that all police officers are not bad and that the officers killed in Dallas, Texas might have had families and children of their own who struggle with their own tragic losses and questions.

Not a day goes by that I don't think about the heartache caused by the accountability intended to correct the wrong done in these violent crimes and family tragedies. As a victim searching for my own understanding, I have participated in support groups that share my story, but I already know my story. Yet, I still deeply desire to understand, which requires me to learn from the stories of those around me.

Moving beyond tragedy takes courage, sacrifice, and a willingness to learn about the commonalities in losses that can bring us together. The need to break this cycle cannot be more urgent than it is today. Families and communities coming together after tragedy need to find ways to celebrate the lives of those they've lost, through common elements of character and humanity often overshadowed by misunderstandings and judgments. Sharing the most important and special stories that depict our loved ones' humanity is a necessary first step toward building bridges.

We must build bridges through compassion, empathy and positive examples of human spirit. We must see the humanity in each other, not simply skin colour. It is here that we develop and maintain trust and respect. If we cannot do these things we will regress to our narratives of good versus evil; to the stories that determine someone was the guilty one.

Breaking from the old narrative through dialogue and building new stories and experiences together allows leaders, communities and a new generation to bridge differences through shared human experiences. Together we must learn to share our stories. There is greatness in each survivor, in every community, to share and celebrate the people they loved with the intention of impacting the human spirit. Together we can rewrite the narrative for future generations.

JEMIMAH L. YOUNG

20. UNDER-EDUCATED AND OVER-ADJUDICATED

Our world changed following the deaths and brutality of Black men and women, caught in graphic detail on cell phones. The deaths of unarmed Black men and women, has initiated a renewed examination of race relations between Black and White Americans. The only difference between today and events of the past is that the advent of technology allows citizens to record these atrocities. The current climate in the United States (U.S.) conveys a very clear and adversative message to the Black community.

The unfailing truth is that Black lives do not matter, and have not mattered in the United States, which can be seen in the many deplorable realities of the Black existence in our society. Specifically, the social, emotional, psychological, economic, and physical well-being of Black people pales in comparison to that of other racial groups. U.S. society touts education as the great equalizer for the disadvantaged. Black students, however, rank last in every educational skill category in schools. They rank first in the frequency and severity of school disciplinary infractions. If schools are to be the great equalizer, they must serve students equitably.

Black people are not protected or served by the justice or educational systems dedicated to their communities. For instance, Black students are overrepresented in special education, underrepresented in gifted education, and disciplined at a higher rate. Similarly, Black citizens are detained, harassed, arrested, and killed by the police at a higher rate than other racial groups. These trends represent the many lived experiences of Black Americans that inform their perceptions of teachers and police officers.

For many Black families, the reality is that teachers lack cultural competence and fail to understand the unique needs of children of colour – namely Black children. Police officers, similarly, often profile and stereotype Black people, leading to confrontational, hostile, and hyper vigilant interactions, which in turn makes Black people feel anxious, threatened, and unsafe. These depictions of teachers and police officers are in stark contrast to the characterizations constructed by mainstream society. According to mainstream thought, teachers and police officers are revered public servants. Teachers educate and care for our most precious resources – children, while police officers are supposed to keep us safe. However, these positive portraits reflect experiences with teachers and police officers that many Black people in America lack.

OVER-ADJUDICATION

One unique aspect of the policing profession is discretion. This discretion, unfortunately, is not colour-blind, and tends to only afford White perpetrators the *benefit of the doubt*. Several years ago, I witnessed the colour of discretion in school disciplinary actions. At the time, my school enacted an active "zero tolerance" policy. Zero tolerance usually applies to drugs, alcohol, threats, and weapons. According to zero tolerance policies schools must levy consequences "no matter what." In my example, the first student was a White male that had a hunting rifle in the back of his truck that he forgot to remove after a weekend hunting trip.

While the rifle was unloaded, the ammunition was in the vehicle in plain sight. The second student, a Black male, had an open container of liquor that he hid in his backpack because his mother was alcohol dependent and he wanted to limit her intake over the weekend. In this situation, the young, White, affluent honour student received the *benefit of the doubt*. The school notified the parents, and they came and removed the rifle. In the other situation, the young Black student experiencing abject poverty was sent to an alternative school. Both of these instances happened at the same school, in the same week, and both were violations in accordance with the school's "zero tolerance" policy.

When this story reached the media, school administrators justified the differential execution of the policy on the fact that the rifle was not "inside" the school (it was confiscated from the student's truck), while a teacher noticed the alcohol when the student opened his backpack in class. As an educator, I found myself perplexed with this logic, given the student parking lot is part of the school premises, and that the harm a rifle could inflict is much more severe than alcohol.

The police officers used their discretion to resolve the issue as they saw most appropriate. In this example, providing the proximity/location of the gun as context to the situation is precisely the type of contextual evidence that zero tolerance seeks to dismiss. These types of inequitable and discriminatory practices are mitigating factors to the over-adjudication that results from the school-to-prison pipeline. These inequitable disciplinary actions perpetuate the lack of trust between the Black community, schools, and police officers.

UNDER-EDUCATION: EXTRA SPECIAL EDUCATION

This narrative involves a former student that I will refer to as Jakobe. Jakobe transferred into my class after hurricane Katrina forced his family to relocate. Jakobe was a high school junior with good overall grades from his former school, but when he transferred to Texas he was subjected to "our" standardized testing protocol as a requirement for graduation.

This is important to note because the curriculum in Texas and Louisiana are quite different. In each respective state teachers, often 'teach to the test' from elementary school to high school, placing Jakobe at a disadvantage. Nonetheless, Jakobe was able to pass his mathematics, science, and language arts exams with relative ease. He struggled, however, to pass the social studies exam. In the state of Texas, students had to pass their social studies exit exam in order to graduate. His struggles were a by-product of his move from Louisiana. Jakobe struggled in the areas of Texas history and world Geography (taught from a Texas Eurocentric/Egocentric perspective).

Jakobe continued to struggle in this area, which prompted administrators to have him tested for special education. They argued this was as a means to "help him" while they helped themselves by reducing their annual failure rate. Despite passing all of the other content areas and his lack of exposure to this information, he was ushered into special education.

The unnecessary placement of Black students in special education is detrimental to the construction of positive academic identities in the Black community. Similarly, inhibiting their access to gifted and advanced placement course work has the same effect. Black students are under-educated by our educational system, which tends to give Black students lifelong labels that can limit their ability to reach their full potential.

Some examples include *culturally deprived, emotionally disturbed*, or *aggressive*. Jakobe, in retrospect, and all the other students from Louisiana should have been exempt from the exam process given the inherent disadvantage they encountered from their sudden and traumatic displacement. If these displaced students were White, I suspect that administrators would move mountains to support the maintenance of their academic identity. I watched that school year and the next, as more than half of the students that originally transferred into my class slowly funnelled into special education programs. What is truly disheartening in this situation was the appreciation some Black families expressed. They believed what that administration presented as an approach to help their children graduate.

WHOSE LIVES REALLY MATTER?

These proceeding vignettes are only two of the many stories of how schools and law enforcement agencies work in concert to push young Black people into 'the system' early and often. Even when we consider the taught curriculum, there are gaping flaws in content delivery and presentation. Students of colour are taught about the "right to vote," and that our Electoral College system is based on being representative of the individual states.

Unfortunately, the current voting system was heavily influenced by the Three-Fifths Compromise of 1787, which states that slaves were counted as three-fifths a person, creating more votes for their White slave owners to vote for their preferred officials during election time. This laid the foundation for the Electoral College system we have today – that many falsely believe is representative and democratic. These trends of disservice and indifference are commonplace in the U.S. educational system.

The inadequacies of these characterizations require a critical examination to place them in a more inclusive context throughout our curriculum and standardized assessment protocols. Black students remain under-educated literally and figuratively. The lack of opportunities to learn in schools serving Black students is enduring.

Subsequently, the under-education of Black children is a direct indication that their lives do not matter, or rather only matter three-fifths as much. Thus, the actualized learning of Black students is "three-fifths" of what America provides to other racial groups. This lack of opportunity in the land of opportunity is a longstanding by-product of the under-education of Black students.

With respect to the school to prison pipeline, as more states are considering stricter rules and expanded zero tolerance initiatives, this pipeline becomes more fluid. School fighting is now a class E felony according to Missouri law. Class E felonies can result in up to four years in prison, and disqualify students from financial aid. In context, this means that if a 2nd grader gets into a fight, they can earn a felony assault record before they can fully comprehend the gravity of the consequences (e.g. Cook County, Illinois).

Like most laws, policies, and rules in the U.S., the execution of this law will be at the discretion of educators and law enforcement officials that often lack the cultural competence to make objective decisions despite their preponderance with colour-blind ideologies. To redress the school-to-prison pipeline those who adjudicate situations must be better educated. Without better education, the over-adjudication of Black children will persist.

Much of the anti-Black Lives Matter rhetoric focuses on an adoption of the mantra All Lives Matter. In reality all lives do matter, however some matter more and some matter less. Black lives matter more to the prison industrial complex compared to the U.S. educational system. Thus, it often seems as if schools and law enforcement work in tandem to keep Black bodies in the school-to-prison pipeline.

It is easier to under-educate and over-adjudicate individuals that live outside your community. Many teachers and police officers live in homogenous White communities, located in distant locations from the communities they serve. This lack of proximity prevents police officers and teachers from fully immersing themselves in Black communities as public servants. For example, if your students are not your neighbours you can disassociate from their failures because they are not part of your community.

Likewise, since Tyrone, Jamaal, or Malcom do not attend your church or have kids that play on the same baseball team as your kids it does not matter, whether they go home to their families because you will not miss them. They are considered work related challenges or concerns – not people. Because police officers and teachers tend not to live in the communities they serve, they also tend to overlooked shared lived experiences and basic commonalities that emerge as people interact as members of a community.

Teachers and police officers should begin to immerse themselves in the communities they serve. They should practice regular introspection to evaluate how their actions may contribute to the demise of young Black men and women in the communities they serve. It is important that educational and judicial systems recognize that Black lives matter in the classroom and in the community. This is the first step toward reversing the under-education and over-adjudication of Black people in the U.S.

REBECCA A. NEAL AND IDARA ESSIEN

21. THE ROLE OF FAITH IN ADVOCATING FOR BLACK MINDS

Regardless of the circumstances in school or society, it is evident that Black people, particularly Black males, are often criminalized. This criminalization can lead to people being adversely impacted by a ubiquitous devaluing of Black lives. Black Lives Matter represents an emphatic statement saying "Black Lives Matter *Too*" – not more than others, and certainly not less than others. They matter to the same degree that other lives do, or at least they should.

In a society that denigrates Black people, however, the assertion that Black Lives Matter must be made to help demonstrate the validity of a value that is not widely held. Of course, most agree with the notion that Black Lives Matter, at least in theory. But theory divorced from action is misguided at best, and self-deception at worst. Belief must be met with action.

The Black Lives Matter movement helps to translate these same concerns to educational settings. Often in schools, Black children are disproportionately represented in special education, overrepresented in schools' exclusionary discipline practices. Frequently, this kind of *pushout* starts in early childhood setting and often becomes school and life trajectories for Black students.

This reality begs the question, do educators truly believe that Black Lives and Minds Matter? The conditions of the educational experiences of Black youth may suggest otherwise. We argue that one cannot value Black minds unless the lives of Black people are cared for. How can one value the mind if they do not value the life?

Our research and practice as educators is motivated by the goal of expressing the value of Black lives and minds. Though we are representative of several fields of study, including early childhood postsecondary education (Idara Essien), special education and postsecondary education (Rebecca Neal), our intellectual spaces within these fields focus on Black learners.

A salient theme across our work is the notion that educators must validate students, express authentic care, centre learning within their lived socio-cultural experiences, and convey high expectations for student achievement performance. While the educational research literature is certainly attentive to these topics, our goal in advocating for these principles emanates from another source, our faith.

While we identify as scholars of colour, our identities are also directly tied to our collective Christian faith, spirituality, and religiosity. These concepts refer to our belief in God (faith), our connection to the spiritual realm (spirituality), and the manner in which we live and carry out that faith (religiosity). Our faith teaches us that children and those who are downtrodden by society are to be supported and protected.

In particular, the Christian religion teaches us to protect and nurture children. In Matthew 18, verse 5, Jesus instructed his followers by stating "And anyone who welcomes a little child like this on my behalf is welcoming me." In the subsequent verse, a warning is provided to anyone who would treat a child in a manner that would take them off of a righteous path.

As faith-based scholars of colour, we view this verse (and many others) as a clarion call to humanize educational experiences. We also use this verse to guide us in how to produce outcomes for our children and youth that are desirable. This represents the translation of the spiritual context to the academic context, where the same concept is applied in different spaces, in different ways.

Although the manner in which some in the Black Lives Movement advocate for similar principles differ; often it is based on the level of anger associated with the mistreatment of Black people. However, this anger can lead to very different places. Here is a collective reflection on resolving this anger in fruitful ways:

> Right now, there are many people who are angry. And anger in and of itself is not bad. But anger leads to two diverging paths, it can lead to hate, and hate only destroys, lowers, and hurts. The other path is righteous indignation, where our anger is harnessed to provoke direct action that remediates the factors that have given rise to our anger. We must choose our paths wisely, as they lead to very different places, and there is nothing worse than choosing a path that leads us to make decisions we cannot change.

Education at all levels should provide students with a safe haven to learn. However, for some Black students, schools are not safe havens. In these settings, some schools are commonly more aptly viewed as battlefields where learners are repeatedly exposed to disparate experiences, conditions, and outcomes.

Often, these challenges begin early on, during the formative years of schooling in early childhood and continue throughout students' educational pathways. While some students will successfully traverse the numerous pitfalls that await them, many will be pushed out along the way. Whether this attrition occurs in elementary, junior high, high school, or college, the reality is that far too few Black students succeed in the American educational system.

There are a number of reasons why this occurs. For some, the challenge of school success is compounded by life conditions such as financial pressures, family concerns, or even stressful life events (such as food and housing insecurities). Harmfully, these pressures are often cited by teachers and faculty who educate Black students as the primary factors limiting their success.

Understanding students through such a deficit lens increases the prevalence of negative racial stereotypes regarding Black students which cannot be ignored. These stereotypes fall into a number of categories, but are most simply described as erroneous assumptions that portray Black learners as being academically inferior, having a deviant persona, deriving from cultures that are apathetic, and successes that are solely confined to athletic pursuits.

Beyond these challenges, many Black learners are also taught by educators who have little to no formal training in teaching students of colour. Further, there can be lack of knowledge in those educators understanding the nuances and within group differences of Black communities. Such a lack of understanding is only intensified by the inadequate educational preparation and performance of educators who typically teach Black children, youth, and adults.

While in years past, these trends may have been glossed over and ignored, more attention is being paid to the plight of Black learners. Highlighted is the criminalized manner in which these learners are portrayed. Largely, this attention is a function of increased Black vigilance around the nation and heightened levels of resistance due to the rise of the Black Lives Matter movement.

Trayvon Martin, Michael Brown, Yvette Smith, Tamir Rice, Oscar Grant III, Eric Garner, Freddie Gray, Walter Scott, Alton Sterling, Tanisha Anderson, Philando Castile, Alfred Olongo, and Sandra Bland. These are a few of the numerous names of Black women and men who have been killed at the hands of law enforcement and those in positions of authority. Sadly, many nameless Black students also die a metaphoric death as a result of their derisory school experiences.

Classrooms are the intersection where research, policy and practice meet. However, instead of a harmonious existence, a crash has occurred leaving Black students *disabled*. In a broader sense, schools have become an educational battlefield that places teachers and Black students on the front lines where these students are coming home *wounded* from not being taught at school or *losing their lives* to (mis) education.

Challenges of Black youth and young adults are unlike any other student. The state of education for Black students can easily be described as precarious, grim, and at times seemingly hopeless. Students are *dying in record numbers to the 'bullets' of overrepresentation in special education and disproportionate representation in school discipline* being aimed at them. Beyond school, other *'bullets'* being aimed at Black students are poverty, low teacher expectations and the deadliest of them all, *the expectation of school and life failure.*

Adding to the complexity of students' school experiences, Black children hear negative associations to the word black: black hole, black market, blackball, blacklisted, blackmail (black male), and the like. Understanding that word associations can positively or negatively influence a child's identity, the vignette presented describes one teacher's intentional practice to positively shape self-image of kindergarten age students in special education attending an urban school.

Mr. Reed, a kindergarten teacher is coloring with his students when he hears students talking about how ugly the colors black and brown are. Black is ugly. I don't want black. I don't want black either. Yuck. Brown is yucky too. I don't want brown either. Listening to the children, and understanding that Black also a cultural referent, Mr. Reed intentionally makes positive associations to the terms black and brown. During coloring time, he can regularly be heard saying how much he loves black and brown, and that those are his two favorite colors. This behavior and language is also modeled by the other adults in the classroom. As the school year continues, Mr. Reed notices students change their narrative and begin indicating that black and brown are appealing colors. Although Mr. Reed's associations to black and brown can easily been seen as trivial, he was intentional in how he worked to disrupt students' negative connotations of black and brown. By the end of the school year, it warmed Mr. Reed's heart to hear the students say, how much they loved black and brown.

Despite the consistent mistreatment of Black learners by educators and the negative constructions of Black identities, our faith encourages us to take a second path, one of righteous indignation. We are taught to love ourselves, and both our enemies and our neighbours. Emboldened by our faith, we believe that all educators should be engaged with tone of acceptance, love, and positive self-imagery. We embrace difficult conversations and address subliminal messaging on educational injustice from this standpoint.

Our faith and research enables us to better understand the role that racism and stereotypes plays on the educational experiences of Black learners. The deleterious outcomes of minoritizing education require that we engage educators in critical conversations on the role of implicit bias, privilege, advantage, and micro aggressions. Such discourse is certainly not comfortable, however, a love for educators and for learners requires that our belief in the detrimental nature of most cross-racial interactions is met with action that tries to create better student experiences.

These challenges represent the need to change hearts and perspectives of Black children. The current condition of education is a heart condition; educator's actions are an outgrowth of their hearts. We believe the vast majority of educators want to better educate and support Black learners. The challenge is not a function of a lack of care, but instead a lack of understanding of what to do. Educators must be taught about the importance of cultural relevancy, collaborative learning, and anti-deficit perspectives. It is essential that we begin to better provide these educators with strategies and practices that can work to improve outcomes for Black students.

AMBER C. BRYANT

22. BLACK LIVES MATTER, BUT ONLY SO MUCH?

Evaluating Per Pupil Expenditures in Two Detroit
Metropolitan School Districts

The *Black Lives Matter* (BLM) movement advocates for several main tenets: diversity, globalism, loving engagement, collective value, and empathy. BLM movement intends to increase unification among African American communities as well as to promote critical awareness of racial disparity issues throughout American society. In keeping with the spirit of the movement, this chapter seeks to bring awareness of per pupil expenditures on instructional services in combination with racial compositions of urban schools.

This focus here is a discussion race and the per pupil expenditures of two school districts within the Detroit metropolitan area, Detroit City Schools (DPS) and Bloomfield (BH) public school districts. These two districts are close in geographic proximity (i.e., within 30 miles of each other) yet differ greatly in academic achievement outcomes and allocation of financial resources. DPS is the largest school district in the state of Michigan, with the highest number of students enrolled (approx. 43,000). BH is ranked 57th on the same list (approx. 5,000 students).

Throughout the chapter, I will shed light on the financial inequities present in these urban school environments and the potential impact they have on student achievement. This research supports the claim that racial segregation and funding inequities can be contributors to gaps in academic achievement between Black and White students in Southeast Michigan. In order to better understand this claim, first, this chapter provides a brief history of federal and Michigan state legislation as it relates to education, a summary of per pupil expenditures in the aforementioned districts, implications of the findings, and recommendations for future reform.

A BRIEF HISTORY

In 1966, the Coleman Report was published by Congress and drew from over 4,000 schools and 600,000 students grades 1–12 laying a foundation for much of the educational policy that we have today. The report's biggest claim was that family structure and family background were the most influential factors on student academic achievement. No research of this magnitude has been conducted on this topic since, and its narrative involving family background continues to legitimatize policies throughout urban cities.

© KONINKLIJKE BRILL NV, LEIDEN, 2018 | DOI 10.1163/9789004378735_022

Additionally, the Coleman Report highlighted disproportionate academic outcomes between Black and White students involved in the study. Since then, *No Child Left Behind* has provided us with more rigorous findings with regard to academic achievement throughout the country. One benefit of these two political agents has been increased data collection for analysis of racial disparities present throughout our nation's public schools.

Because the Coleman Report and *No Child Left Behind* (NCLB) both had national policy implications, the state of Michigan was not immune to their repercussions. Detroit's student achievement was so consistently low it was taken over by the state government in 1999 and has been run by a stream of emergency managers. Emergency managers, traditionally from political science or business-related fields, have primary goals of balancing deficit budgets and developing action plans for district recovery. Detroit public schools are chronically underfunded, meaning that the schools lack resources and struggle to offer competitive teacher pay.

Historical patterns of racial segregation and economic isolation have left the city of Detroit unable to maintain adequate water supply, public electricity, public safety, or high-quality public schooling. Surrounding neighborhoods and cities, like Bloomfield Hills, house the residents and descendants of residents who participated in *white flight* during the mid-1900s. For example, in 1910, Detroit was approximately 99% White. By the turn of the 21st century, the population was over 80% African American.

In 2009, the *Detroit Free Press* reported that more than 50% of the city's adult residents were functionally illiterate. In 2013, *Forbes* deemed Detroit the #1 most miserable city in America. It is the most impoverished city in the country and recently declared the municipal largest bankruptcy in American history. Today, urban areas that suffered from mass exodus of their tax-paying middle-class residents are struggling to regain economic stability, and generational poverty persists.

BH is situated in Oakland County, the second wealthiest county per capita of counties over one million people in the United States. In 2000, became the first county in Michigan with property wealth exceeding $100 billion. BH is over 85% White, with a population of over 41,000 residents. The county's over 53,000 businesses produce a combined annual payroll with a GDP higher than 19 states ($26.6 billion).

It is evident that the racial and economic compositions of these two cities counter each other dramatically, which has greater social implication than the differences between urban and suburban physical environments. Research has shown that urban cities have less financial support than necessary to ensure equitable conditions in schools in comparison to their suburban counterparts. These resource differences and the community environments that result (or maybe even produce) them have grave implications for a county's economic stability.

PER PUPIL EXPENDITURES

Per pupil expenditure is the amount spent on each student to provide instruction, instructional staff services, student support, operation and maintenance, administration, transportation, and food services. Publically available data suggest that the total expenditure for education per pupil in DPS 2014–2015 was $16,347.83 and for BH, $29,921.54 – a 45.4% difference. Annual state and federal revenue provided per pupil is similar in both districts ($18,602 in DPS; $18,032 in BH). The non-instructional services, such as food operations and other uses, takes up 494% more of the budget for DPS than BH ($5,077 per pupil compared to $855, respectively).

BH has 12 total schools. 80% of the students in the district are considered proficient in math and/or reading and their have a graduation rate of 96%, 14% higher than the national average. The annual budget is over $100 million and 8% of the school district receives free or reduced lunch. DPS has 97 schools. 30% of the students in the district are proficient in math and or reading and the graduation rate is 65%, 19% lower than the national average. The annual budget for DPS is over $1.2 billion, and 82% of students are receiving free or reduced lunch. Researchers, drawing on statistics like these, should better analyze differences in education as it relates to race, finances, and residential advantages.

IMPLICATIONS AND RECOMMENDATIONS

BlackLivesMatters' tenets of diversity, globalism, loving engagement, collective value, and empathy are principles of inclusive solutions that can address educational inequities in urban schools. The assumption here is that education has the potential to help equalize ethnic and economic disparities in our country. Educational equity might best be viewed as a sound and fruitful investment in responding to political pressures and lobbying outcomes.

High-quality public schools are an investment for all. President Obama once explain that for every $1 invested in early childhood education, $7 is spared in later years for welfare and social service benefits. Since 2016, BLM has proven itself to be a mass mobilizing change-agent for many young Americans, both Black and White, around the country. As prior movements have proven, effective and persistent non-violent resistance is worthy. BLM is a platform for conversations such as these on ethnic educational equities.

When discussing per pupil expenditures, due to the varying needs of children, financial allocations should be based on needs assessments and addressed at the state and local levels through aggressive and explicit legislative changes. Exemplar city Louisville, KY, provides a model for increased equity across city limits. Louisville created a city-county merger that revitalized and sustains its most disadvantaged communities. The city-county system illustrates some of the most consistently positive reform in public schools in the country.

In 1972, Louisville established a city-county model where adjoining counties support one another through funding and inter-county bussing; these were the same doctrines of those fighting in favor of *Milliken v. Bradley* in Detroit. However, Louisville was able to establish a city-county district, while Detroit split into two racially-divided halves.

In 2010, these two cities had the same percentage of Black residents. The average black Detroit student, however went to school with less than two percent white students, while in Louisville, the average black student went to a school that was half white. In 2011, 62 percent of Louisville fourth graders were at or above proficiency in math, with only 31 percent of Detroit's students.

The point here is not that the presence of White children is a prerequisite to academic improvement. Rather, intentional political and organizational structures are necessary to better academic proficiency for all students. Further examination is needed in regard to per pupil spending and achievement as research results have been inconclusive in recent studies; nevertheless, money as a factor is never really be excluded from the conversation.

Solutions to address per pupil spending in Detroit and other urban districts must include legislative support. Solutions must also draw upon the inclusion of stable surrounding districts. In order to gain the necessary momentum behind this cause, all stakeholders must agree that it is the children's best interest that we serve and this, in turn, is truly in the best interest of everyone.

LAWRENCE BAINES, JENNIE HANNA AND STACEY HUGHES

23. US VERSUS THEM

Charter Schools, Vouchers, and the New Segregation

During his reign as Secretary of Education, Arne Duncan was one of the country's most ardent advocates for charter schools. Duncan's persistent and aggressive support of charters translated into billions of dollars of federal funding and escalating charter school enrolments. Today, there are 6,700 charter schools scattered among 43 states, with total enrolment nearing three million.

The unprecedented federal funding streams earmarked for charter schools over the past eight years have been supplemented by billions of dollars from private philanthropists, including the Bill and Melinda Gates Foundation, the Eli Broad Foundation, the Koch Family Foundations, the Walton Foundation, and others. While charter school advocates, such as The National Alliance of Public Charter Schools, herald the superiority of charter schools, the research base supporting gains in achievement, improvements in student dispositions, or improved integrity of character over that of "traditional" public schools is, at best, inconclusive.

One of the effects of charter schools that might be considered deleterious is their tendency to segregate students into environments where they only encounter peers who look, think, speak, and act just like they do. Four examples of charter schools designed to attract students with specific racial, religious, or academic characteristics include: (1) Iften School, (2) Ben Gamla Charter, (3) Native American Community Academy, and (4) the Betty Shabazz International Charter school. All four are publicly supported charter schools.

The Iftin School in San Diego is exclusively Muslim, and most students are from Somalia. Indeed, the school was founded by refugees from Somalia. Several photos from the school's website show girls standing around at recess in their hijabs, while boys romp around on the playground behind them.

Students at the Ben Gamla Charter School in Florida are almost exclusively Jewish and white. The school requires Hebrew language immersion and offers a curriculum heavily influenced by Israeli culture. The Native American Community Academy in Albuquerque was expressly created for Native American students with a curriculum emphasizing Native American perspectives. Meanwhile, at the Betty Shabazz International Charter School in Chicago, students are all African-American and the school infuses elements of African culture.

Of these four charter schools, two are overtly religious – Iftin is Muslim, Ben Gamla is Jewish – and all four mandate a curriculum that is explicitly outside

© KONINKLIJKE BRILL NV, LEIDEN, 2018 | DOI 10.1163/9789004378735_023

of the traditional American curriculum. Iftin embraces Somalian cultural norms, Ben Gamla takes inspiration from Israel, NACA fosters Native American culture and beliefs, and Betty Shabazz looks to Africa for inspiration and curricular grounding.

The advantages of diverse schools and classrooms are well established. Current educational policies promulgated by the federal government and supported by private philanthropists, and fuelled by profit-hungry entrepreneurs, however, have advocated for the abandonment of neighbourhood public schools as a social good. The splintering of public school populations into distinctive, independent islands is in opposition to the idea of the free and open common school developed in the U.S. during the 19th century.

In the 19th century, it was thought that public schools in America would be places of equal opportunity. The idea of a free and public education was that wealthy and poor would meet in common purpose. Public schools would be places where recognition and rewards would be gained through genuine merit and not meted out according to social class. Public schools were to build character, impart knowledge, and valorise democratic ideals.

While publicly-funded charter schools are prohibited from discrimination through federal statues, such as Title VI of the Civil Rights Act, the Individuals with Disabilities Education Act (IDEA), and Title IX of the Education Amendments Act of 1972, even a cursory investigation of these schools reveals that many are selective. While charter schools may not overtly discriminate in admissions policies, many are de-facto segregated schools with curricula aligned to specific religious or cultural principles. As a result, publicly-funded charter schools are among the most segregated campuses in the nation.

THE RISE OF VOUCHERS

One of the first proponents of school vouchers was economist Milton Friedman. In 1955 he claimed that parents should be able to use public funds to pay for the school of their choice. Today, vouchers, tuition tax credits, and education savings accounts can be found in 27 states. Recent studies, however, have found that students who go to private schools via vouchers suffer academically. Despite the underwhelming performance of students who attend private schools through voucher programs, new Secretary of Education Betsy DeVos has repeatedly stated her disdain for open-enrolment public schools, calling them "dead ends" and "failures."

While one of the defining characteristics of the United States always has been its diversity, the organization of the school system (public urban, suburban, and rural; publicly-funded charter and private schools) has aided and abetted the continuing segregation of students. Secretary DeVos' antagonistic, anti-public school stance is not unique. It could be argued that, in recent years, the most powerful educational organization in the country – the U.S. Department of Education – has been the primary incubator and enforcer of neo-liberal, anti-public school policies.

One wonders about the long-term effects of the continued filtering of children into hermetically-sealed schools, each with its very own, custom-made curricula and neatly-charted profitability projections. The places where all Americans come to meet in common purpose have been disintegrating for decades, aided in no small part by the relentless flurry of governmental mandates that have slashed funding for programs associated with improving the quality of life for every American, "the common good."

Many services, such as national defence, rehabilitation services, highways, water utilities, sanitation, parks and recreation, and public health have already been auctioned off to the highest bidders. In 2016, the ratio of private military contractors to American soldiers in Afghanistan was 3:1; one hundred percent of Florida's juvenile prisons are now private, for-profit businesses; a Spanish corporation now owns $8 billion worth of assets and hundreds of miles of American highway. The list of formerly public enterprises created for the common good that have been bought and sold grows at breakneck speed. Public schools are simply the next target.

In the midst of the privatization blitzkrieg, perhaps it is a small miracle that public schools in America have survived at all. Unlike businesses and corporations, most public schools cannot afford to pay lobbyists and public relations firms to influence public opinion and policy. They instead quietly bear lambasting from critics, governmental *redirection* of billions of dollars of public funding into the coffers of education profiteers, and the flight of philanthropists from public schools to boutique, largely segregated charter/private schools.

Historically, proponents of segregation have treated the inclusive nature of public schools as a fatal flaw. Every time the doors of public schools have been opened a little wider – to welcome women, the poor, black students, immigrants, and children with special needs – proponents of segregation have proclaimed the end of public schools.

Public schools educate 47 million (90%) of U.S. school-aged students. They do this work despite decreases in funding, the unremitting onslaught of new governmental regulations, impossible accountability targets, and ever-higher expectations. 47 million might seem like a lot, especially considering that the policies, money, and momentum of the past three decades have favoured the 10% over the 90%.

47 million children, however, may not be enough to slow the privatization juggernaut. By stripping money and autonomy from public education under the guise of choice, DeVos and the U.S. Department of Education are doing their part to bury free and open public schools. The goal seems to be to build a wall around the 10%, and have the 90% pay for it.

KERRI J. TOBIN AND STEPHEN M. LENTZ

24. POLICING THE SCHOOL

"It wasn't supposed to happen like that!" An email from a distressed graduate student details an event that happened at his student teaching placement: a seventh-grade student was caught with a cell phone, in clear violation of school rules. The student teacher and another young teacher confronted the student and took the phone from him. The student grabbed the phone back from the teacher and pushed past him, refusing to come back and surrender the phone.

The teachers decided to report the incident to their administrator, thinking the student would serve a detention for breaking a school rule. What happened shocked them both: the administrators called the police, filed an assault charge, and the student was led out of the school in handcuffs. The student teacher was dumbfounded, the guilt he felt at having been part of the situation palpable in the email he sent detailing the incident. "I had no idea they were going to call the police! He didn't assault anybody!"

What went on here? Why would an administrator involve the police over a grabbed cell phone? And why would the police take such a charge seriously, responding by arresting a 12-year-old child and removing him in handcuffs? The incident described above, unfortunately, is not an uncommon one, but it is instructive when we think about how relationships between communities and police forces become strained, how trust is lost, and where opportunities for repair are squandered.

DEMOGRAPHICS AND BIAS

It is important to examine demographics in incidents like these. In the above scenario, the student was an African American male from a low-SES background attending school in a predominantly wealthy white district. These interactions are not unusual, in that most administrators and police officers, like most Americans, harbor implicit biases that impact the ways they view people of colour. Classroom misbehaviour is more likely to be labelled disruptive or threatening when students are African American and the teacher is white.

Likewise, white people consistently overestimate the age of African American children by an average of five years. So, when a white assistant principal looks at a 12-yr-old African American student, his subconscious tells him that person is 17, which makes him expect 17-year-old self-control capacity, rather than the trademark impulsivity of a 12-year-old. This disconnect makes him believe the student is out of control – not behaving appropriately. When combined with likely subconscious racial bias assuming African American students are predisposed to unruly or criminal behaviour, the administrator's response becomes predictable.

SOCIAL AND POLITICAL ATMOSPHERE

Readers over a certain age may remember when a time in school when the police were never called. There was a time before school resource officers (a euphemism for armed police officers) had become an ordinary part of the backdrop of public schooling in the United States. We also went to school in a time before what is now called accountability, in which schools operate under fear of financial and personnel penalties for student test scores.

A common assumption on the part of teachers and administrators is that disruptive students bring down overall test score averages, and to expel those students raises test scores. A school resource officer (SRO) at one high-performing high school in Northeastern Pennsylvania told a district attorney there that the principal's intention was to "get rid of the bad kids" by having them arrested. This would give the school administration grounds to expel them.

This particular principal sometimes even went as far as to put pressure on the school resource officer – an officer of the law – to try to get him to charge students with crimes even when the SRO did not believe the charges were warranted. In one such case, the school resource officer became concerned and contacted the district attorney's office to ask for guidance, and was told that he should use his professional judgment, not the principal's, to determine whether a crime had been committed.

The officer described above often declined to charge children, but in many other cases, officers bend to the will of the administrators for whom they believe they work. The SRO's role in the U.S. is poorly-defined and poorly-understood, as was made clear in 2015 when video of a South Carolina high schooler being violently thrown on the floor and dragged out of a classroom by an SRO – for the crime of not obeying a teacher's order – went viral on the Internet. When does breaking a school rule become a crime? Is an SRO just another administrator, there to enforce school rules, but with the threat of force and criminal penalty?

The student in South Carolina was eventually cleared, and the officer was fired, but questions of who works for whom are often ambiguous. Children's legal rights become dependent upon individual SROs' understandings of their jobs, as well as their personalities, which vary dramatically from officer to officer. Indeed, even judges express frustration with school officials who seem intent on throwing every possible obstacle in front of students trying to returning to school after expulsion. But criminal judges have no jurisdiction over school officials.

In addition to giving administrators grounds to expel students they believe will drag down their test scores, using SROs as a front-line for discipline solves another problem borne of the era of accountability in schools. In this day and age, schools can be penalized if they are seen as taking too many disciplinary actions against students. A school with many suspensions, for example, looks on paper like a place where students are out of control; that school's principal has an incentive to keep detention and suspension numbers down rather than be penalized for maintaining a disorderly school.

The actions of the SRO, however, are not included in tallies, and become a way for schools to enforce rules without being held to account. Consider the case of a high school student in a low-performing urban district in Pennsylvania who took his teacher's pizza and ate it. The principal contacted the SRO and asked that the student be arrested for theft. By the time the SRO contacted the DA's office to ask what to do, the student had paid the teacher back for the pizza. Most telling, the school took no action – no detention, no phone call to parents, preferring instead to have a child arrested for eating someone else's $10 lunch.

LOSS OF TRUST

It is not hard to imagine how the child thrown from her seat and dragged across the floor for normal adolescent misbehaviour in South Carolina will likely suffer trauma and lasting mistrust of police officers as a result of the experience. Likewise, the student charged with assault for grabbing his phone back from a teacher in Louisiana cannot be expected to trust that authorities – legal or educational – have his best interests in mind. In the second case, the student was expelled from school. Some questions that come to mind:

What is our expectation of his life trajectory now?

How does he view himself?

How does society treat a child arrested and kicked out of school at age 12?

How does he go on to develop an adult identity full of the self-confidence and self-love we know are required for successful adulthood?

And what of the student who, perhaps even jokingly, ate his teacher's pizza? Had the SRO gone along with the principal's request and arrested him, what impact would that have had on his life?

One interaction with overzealous, biased administrators and police has likely scarred this child – and his parents – for life.

Research tells us that being arrested for small infractions at school dramatically increases the likelihood that a child becomes involved with the criminal justice system as an adult. It's not hard to imagine that he would become distrustful of authority, particularly the police, in a way that would alter his relationship with law enforcement across his life span. His parents might likewise have difficulty trusting that the police play a benevolent, protective role in society.

The more children in a community who have, or witness, these types of negative experiences with police, the greater the breach of trust. Schools often even expel students for infractions that did not happen in school, and when those students try to return after successfully completing a juvenile program, force them into "alternative" schools instead of allowing them back into their regular programs. How could parents and children fail to see SROs, as police officers, as complicit in this shameful behaviour?

CHANGE IS POSSIBLE

Despite the many problems that overactive administrators and SROs create in schools, there are isolated buildings and districts where educators and police officers have created positive interactions. While far too many schools use their SROs as behaviour management staff, some schools have demonstrated that responsible school leadership greatly reduces the need for police presence in the school. For example, administrators in one large school district in Pennsylvania were concerned about balancing the school's internal process of school discipline with how to include the police in more serious criminal matters that occasionally arose.

To that end, administrators contacted the DA's office and asked for a meeting with the local police to determine the effective boundaries between school discipline and police actions. The very fact that this meeting was initiated was a credit to school leadership and the local police because it demonstrated where effective, ethical administrators and police should begin their relationship within the school: as separate entities that focus on separate issues. One crucial policy and structural difference made the above district function effectively: the local police had a presence in the school, but were not SROs employed by the school. They had complete freedom to make decisions about the nature of their policing without direction or interference from school administration. This is important because where SROs are employed by the schools, the overwhelming majority of issues that SROs deal with do not actually require the presence of a police officer.

As discussed above, does a police officer really need to be called because a student is not following directions in class? Or to phrase it another way: if there had been no SRO in the building, would administrators actually make an outside call to local police to send an officer if a student was misbehaving in class? It is not hard to imagine that the answer to both of those questions is no. The only appropriate role for a police officer in a school – SRO or otherwise – is dealing with actual crimes, not school rule violations.

Schools are communities in more ways than one, so it is not unreasonable to think that having police officers in the building might be valuable for students. Indeed, there are examples of communities where pro-active police officers make valuable contributions to their communities. But more often than not, this comes through a less-is-more approach, where officers interact with people in a daily and routine manner, and arrests are limited to only the most essential situations. The same is certainly true in a school setting.

The aforementioned large school district and the local police came to the mutual understanding that police officers should only be contacted for situations that were truly beyond the authority of school officials. When schools are under-resourced, SROs are often used as additional disciplinarians because there aren't enough school personnel to meet the need. Likewise, when there is a marginalized population of students, whether low-income students or students of colour, relationships with police are likely to be fraught with mistrust from the outset. SROs in schools comprised of traditionally underserved students need to be aware that mistrust is likely, and work that much harder to overcome the subconscious biases they have as well as forge positive relationships with students. The potential for change and healing exists, if schools and police can figure out how to harness it.

JEFF FRANK

25. THE HARDENED HEART

What does it mean to have to make the case that a life matters? What does it mean to be offended by the request? What are we to make of the reality that many people feel that the claim that black lives matter is an affront? A not so obvious response to questions like these might be found in the philosophical problem of scepticism concerning other minds.

In one of its most famous iterations, we find Descartes wondering how he knows that he is not living a dream (or nightmare) where the people around him are convincing human-like machines created by an evil demon. To many, the question of the reality of other humans is absurd. Of course, other people are human: we do not treat our children like machines, we respond to children in ways that we do not respond to our toasters, or our cars or even our pets. Problem solved, right?

Well, maybe. Philosopher Stanley Cavell wants us to wonder: Do we really *respond* to humans differently than we respond to machines or animals? To take a large imaginative leap, think for a moment about the slaveholder in the American south. This man might have a deep devotion to a dog and yet viciously beat a black youth for nothing more than smiling at him in a way he finds offensive.

At the same time, this man would find it strange to take his dog to worship at church; yet, he acknowledges that his slaves should and do worship – and though he may inter his beloved dog, he recognizes that his dog does not have a funeral in the way that his slaves do. So, when we consider the mind of the slaveholder in relation to his thinking on the human, we do find ourselves – I think – back in the problem of scepticism concerning the *reality* of other people.

His slaves both are and are not people: he treats his dog more humanely than his slaves in some instances, and yet he also seems to treat his slaves more humanly than his dog in others. The problem of the humanity of other people is not a problem that can be solved abstractly. We respond to this problem each moment in the ways we recognize or fail to recognize the humanity of other humans in our thoughts, in our actions and in our interactions.

Moving into our present age, the problem of the humanity of other people remains with us, but in potentially more problematic ways. The practice of chattel slavery is now illegal, and so too most forms of segregation. But, when we think about the humanity of humans in our time, I find myself deeply worried.

It is too easy to see something like the black lives matter movement as a problem with a solution rather than something that calls for a human response. Though it

© KONINKLIJKE BRILL NV, LEIDEN, 2018 | DOI 10.1163/9789004378735_025

may not seem that way, the response that *all* lives matter is very much a response that does not want to think, to see, to feel. It wants to solve the problem through equation – black lives matter just like any other – and so nothing happens.

But, if the response that *all* lives matter is given a different slant, we might actually begin to get somewhere. That is, if someone is offended by the call that a black life matters because it provokes us to think about what it would mean for any life to matter, then we are in a far different place than we are with the person who glibly dismisses through equation.

As I write this, I worry that the lives of my children do not matter in the ways they should. I worry about the state of the environment that we are passing on to them; I worry about the tensions and hatred caused by our thoughtless national policies; I worry about the quality of love in their lives. I worry that my children are not being seen and treated as the irreplaceable precious gift that they are – in short, treated as humans – and so I worry that their lives do not matter, or do not matter in the ways they should.

The claim that black lives matter may come as an affront because we do not feel that our lives matter in the ways they should. We do not feel like we are profoundly cared for, that our children will be safe as they struggle to find their identity and live fulfilled lives; that – though hard to admit – various forms of (white) privilege are in fact deadening. Instead of trying to awake from this deadness of spirit, we harden our hearts, and we seek to deny others the humanity that we don't feel.

We need major institutional and legal changes in this country, there is no doubt about this, but we can continue to pass laws and policies that will never lead to transformational change because hearts remain profoundly hardened. Here is a deeply troubling and tragic irony of living in an ostensibly Christian nation: those living white privilege are like so many pharaohs walking around with hardened hearts, not accepting the radical and transformative gift of love that opens us back up to our own humanity by making the effort to free, and freely love, the humanity in others.

Love is not a zero-sum game. It is – as James Baldwin reminds us – not an easy road to walk. Even if we (and when I use we in this paragraph, I am specifically referring to we white Americans) know – or have an intimation that – we need more love in our lives, we can be afraid. Though we want to be freed from our hardened heart, though we want to step into a better world, we can also be afraid of everything that might be stripped away should we finally acknowledge our deep need and our true desire.

We are not perfect, we are not happy, we do not have everything figured out, we are afraid. Because we cannot admit this to ourselves, movements like black lives matter are stinging because they force a confrontation with our fear and hope. Here – in the slain, in the blood of black Americans and the dignity of their resistance and strength in advocating for the human – we are given an opening to say: I cannot understand what it would mean to live in a world where black lives matter because I do not know what it would take to make my own life matter.

I am not claiming that any – or even most – white Americans would accept this as a description of their inner lives, so I can only speak personally and from where I am. Living a decent life, let alone a life of love, is something I see as more and more of a distant accomplishment. It is not something I can claim as a birthright of being white, but something I must fight for, and see fleeting away from me at every moment I fail to acknowledge humanity: my own and the humanity of others.

Most specifically, I am an educator, and I confront the humanity of my students every day, and I can meet that humanity or deny it. For me it was a waking up to see that morality was not some grand drama, but rather it all hinged on the ways I responded to a student who needed me when I was busy, tired and worried about my own problems. It was in how I responded to the humanity of that student, in that moment, that mattered. I could acknowledge that student's life as mattering through my response, or choose otherwise.

Compounding and complicating any response is the *role* that we find ourselves in. In addition to responding as a person, I am responding as a teacher. When I talk to other teachers, I sometimes worry that the role has gotten the better of the person. That is, when some teachers talk about students, the tone is almost adversarial: that students need to be watched, controlled, distrusted and – in some cases – feared. The role of the teacher – and the policies that further constrain that role (high-stakes testing, no excuses discipline) – can come to choke out the humanity of the person teaching.

If a role can confound the person in ways that make her less fully human to her students, and a teacher is someone in a helping profession, think about the person who polices. What does the role of being in the police do to the humanity of the person in the role? Former Obama Administration Attorney General Eric Holder made the important point that police are doing the will of those with power. During slavery, they enforced slavery; during segregation, they enforced segregation; given the rhetoric of the super-predator, they treated young black men as inhuman. The role of power cast the humanity of the police into a mold, meant to dehumanize.

The dehumanization goes both ways, to the police and the policed. We have to wonder what the police officer sees when he looks through the eyes of his role and sees a young black man walking down a certain city block. And, we have to wonder what the eyes watching from windows see when they see a police officer driving past their homes. Is the police officer human, or an instrument of institutional racism? Is the young black man human, or is he dispensable; a problem to be dispatched? In this situation, does life matter?

Hearts are hardened. But, not just in the police/policed binary. They are hardened all around. In any of our roles – teacher, parent, lover, spouse, minister, doctor, lawyer – do we respond humanly? When my wife or child is in pain and needs love, do I find ways to provide it, or shirk and shrink this human need? How much more so when it comes to being a white person in a white world? In my role as white, what becomes of my humanity? When a black man looks at me does my whiteness cloud and shroud my humanity, making it impossible for me to respond humanly to black men and women, or in a way that clearly communicates that our lives matter?

These questions show that scepticism concerning other lives should remain a problem unresolved. As a white person, it is often hard to say that black lives matter because we do not know what this means. Until we humanize our white imaginations and educate our responsiveness to the world, black lives will not matter, nor will our own. Instead of assuming I know what it might mean to live as a black American, I try to unlearn my limited perceptions and so attempt to understand the fears, hopes and everydayness of living black and American.

With black lives matter we have an opportunity to reclaim the human, though the hardened heart will certainly not see it that way. How hard our hearts must be when the simple call to treat black lives as if they matter provokes vitriol and not a troubled mind. My mind is troubled, and I hope to learn to be human in the face of all this hate and wasted beauty.

Being human is not a given, it is earned. We must try to make our lives matter by seeing that they never will until we can see what it would mean to live the acknowledgement that black lives matter. Until then we will be stuck living the nightmare of Descartes: inhuman machines living the dream of some evil demon. Black Americans know what this nightmare is like. It is up to us to realize that this nightmare is our creation, dreamt out of our own lack of humanity. Only then will black lives, and our own, matter.

RANDA SULEIMAN AND JIM HOLLAR

26. ALTERNATIVES TO OVERUTILIZING LAW ENFORCEMENT IN OUR SCHOOLS

Hearing from Administrators & Teachers
in Milwaukee County Schools

In Milwaukee, Wisconsin communities of colour and law enforcement have long existed in a relationship marked more by tension than trust. Police in Milwaukee have helped to increase this distrust in recent years, specifically for two incidents involving the deaths of African American suspects while in police custody in 2010 and 2011. In addition, there was a controversy involving illegal strip searches and body cavity searches of 74 African American people by Milwaukee police.

Community members have criticized policing methods in predominantly African American neighbourhoods, which they say often involve a lack of respect towards suspects and use of force. In 2014 community protests in Milwaukee followed the fatal shooting of Dontre Hamilton, a mentally ill African American man. The police officer who killed Hamilton was fired for not following regulations, but was ultimately not charged criminally.

A more recent example of how this erosion of trust has led to violence and unrest occurred in the Sherman Park neighbourhood during the summer of 2016. On August 13, civil disturbances began in Sherman Park in response to the fatal police shooting of Sylville Smith, a 23-year-old African-American male. During the three-day turmoil, several people, including police officers, were injured and dozens of protesters arrested.

The subsequent duelling lawn signs of "Black Lives Matter" and "We Back the Badge" seen across Milwaukee and its surrounding suburbs reflected a gulf in perspectives about law enforcement. The signs also represented makeshift borders. The borders represent a long-established geography of racism: institutionalized segregation within Milwaukee County.

Moreover, Wisconsin as a state has an equally long and dismal record of disproportionate incarceration rates for African American males. The state also ranks last in the nation in both academic achievements gaps between black and white students and suspensions for African American students. Given such entrenched inequities within both state and local contexts, the path forward for Milwaukee, as for many urban centres, must involve a choral re-reading of how we got here, as well as a many-voiced response on how to take the next steps.

© KONINKLIJKE BRILL NV, LEIDEN, 2018 | DOI 10.1163/9789004378735_026

To better understand how the above issues intertwine, this chapter will explore the role of law enforcement inside schools in Milwaukee County. The authors will describe, with the help of former and current administrators and teachers, the relationship between school-based law enforcement and their students. The chapter will also discuss alternatives to law enforcement in schools and how these alternatives may eventually aid in establishing a new level of trust between law enforcement and the communities they serve.

Our first conversation was with a recently retired elementary school principal who worked for more than 20 years. As a teacher and then as a principal of a high-needs school for 15 years, he believed that Milwaukee schools has made efforts to reduce violence and maintain safety across the district by starting preventive practices to reduce violence early in elementary schools. In regards to the efficiency of the School Safety Officer (SSO) program and whether it might be a contributing factor, the principal countered that in his experience, the officers worked hard to build relationships with students and organized programs to get to know them.

He believes students at his former elementary school felt safe with the officers and wanted to spend more time with them doing activities. He describes the officers as resourceful, responsive, and very helpful when it came to legal issues at the school. Over the years and due to their role at the high school, the officers do not have the time to build the relationship with elementary students or do activities with them, as they were needed more and more in the high schools.

We wanted to know more and build a better understanding, so we interviewed another elementary school principal who worked for more than 35 years as a teacher, assistant principal, and principal in high, middle, as well as elementary schools. From his experience, the schools he worked in actively used multiple approaches and implemented various programs to increase safety and reduce violence. Some of these programs were discontinued due to either high cost or inefficiency.

When asked about the involvement of law enforcement, the principal described the "school squads," which are dual-manned police cars that cover a large geographic area and respond to school calls during the school day. The training and experience for these officers prepared them for the position and usually the officer requested the assignment schools they served. Unfortunately, the school squad could be spread pretty thin.

When a school called with a student issue needing police intervention, there was no guarantee that a school squad would respond. The principal said that "there was always the strong hope that a school squad team would be the responders when a call was made." This reflects the strong relationship the officers built with the school administration and the students.

We also reached out to an elementary school teacher who currently serves as teacher leader and has been the coach for the neighbourhood high school volleyball and softball teams for five years. He also serves as an after-school tutor and mentor in the Community Learning Center (CLC) program. He has seen teachers assaulted, hit, kicked and threatened by students. In his fifteen-year career, he has been threatened

108

with violence three times, but luckily, he has not been personally attacked. He believes that this is due to his very calm demeanour and being nice to everyone. He reiterated that the students who that threatened him were very troubled students.

ALTERNATIVES TO TRADITIONAL LAW ENFORCEMENT ACTIONS

One program that this teacher's school has tried to implement to help children cope with anxiety is mindfulness, or the art of learning to relax by breathing. The school has piloted the program for about five years. For the first four years, the school had someone from an outside group called Growing Minds come into the school and give professional development to the staff.

For 2017 the school was on its own, and the teacher was given the task of implementing the mindfulness curriculum. When asked about this program, the teacher said: "Mindfulness is very successful. The kids in my class are very calm. My classroom is very calm. I have a lavender diffuser and meditative music playing daily. I have an aquaponics lab so water is always falling and bubbling."

When asked about possible downfalls, he said: "Like any great program, it needs someone to lead it." He believes that the leader needs to be strong and ready for resistance which most likely will be the teachers as they feel overwhelmed with the multiple initiatives at the school and district level. He thinks that teacher will be hesitant to implement the program because they need to be comfortable with it and they must believe that they can do it effectively. He added that in order for the leader to get teachers buy-in, he must practice it. At the same time, if the teacher teaching Mindfulness does not practice it, the program will fall apart very quickly because the students will not practice it.

Another interesting approach that the teacher has experience with and has seen work is a more concerted effort towards building relationship with students. From his perspective, teachers talked about building relationships, but they normally stopped there. He believed there was not enough training for teachers on how to effectively build relationships with students. He also believed that a longer school day with more CLCs and afterschool programs had helped him build better relationships with students.

We also interviewed a high school teacher who works at one of the academically high-performing high schools in Milwaukee County about his experiences. He said his school focuses more on attendance and academic interventions than other district schools. Part of the school's budget is used to fund three safety members instead of just the two that are provided by the district. In addition, the school has three paraprofessionals who support the school's Comprehensive Behaviour Unit (CBU), which focuses on the highest risk students and their behaviour issues. The CBU is also staffed with two special-education teachers.

In his opinion, there was a correlation at the school between students in need of academic intervention and students that have become violent. Due to his teaching assignment as the tier-2 math interventionist, he shared that he has a relationship with many students who have a higher risk of becoming violent. Teachers as well as

109

three safety staff, three faculty members and the school administration are trained in de-escalating violent outburst. The intervention classroom is customarily used to have students cool-off and the teacher works with them to de-escalate the situation.

Another current alternative to traditional school policing is the use of the Violence Free Zone (VFZ) program to improve student behaviour and academic performance at high-risk middle and high schools. The Milwaukee Violence-Free Zone program is directed by the Washington, D.C.-based Center for Neighborhood Enterprise (CNE) and implemented in Milwaukee schools by CNE's local community partners, the Running Rebels Community Organization and the Milwaukee Christian Center.

VFZ attempts to reduce the number of truancies, suspensions, and violent incidents in public middle and high schools. The Milwaukee VFZ program utilizes Youth Advisers – adults who work full time in the schools as hall and cafeteria monitors, to act as role models and mentors for high risk students. They work closely with school safety officers, teachers, and counsellors to provide an additional support system for students.

One teacher at a high school where the VFZ program is operating reported that in past years there had been an unusual division of responsibilities between school safety aides and School Resource Officers. However, now with VFZ involved with conflict resolution, mediation, small group work, and relationship building, there was more clarity in roles.

One of the principals we interviewed discussed his perspective on the VFZ program and his reservations with it. He said that the program had hired people who lacked the experience to work effectively with students and diffuse volatile situations. In his opinion, program staff spent more time befriending students as a peer than building strong mentoring relationships.

CONCLUSIONS

The perspectives of former and current administrators and teachers are provided here in hopes of starting a larger dialogue on the implications and alternatives to the overutilization of law enforcement within Milwaukee County schools. Although representing only five unique individuals, from an area that employs thousands in both public and private school settings, their perspectives as both insiders and outsiders of communities of colour are insightful. More problematic however, may be their general support for law enforcement in schools.

It also seems as if the alternatives to the presence of law enforcement in schools are often underfunded or distrusted in ways that make reducing the role of law enforcement impractical. To dig into the reasons why police continue to have such a large role in schools would take more space than this brief chapter allows. But it does force the authors to wonder how many administrators and teachers, who work so closely with students of colour, remain bound by the same racially segregated opinions concerning why various communities mistrust their local law enforcement organizations.

JOHN WILLIAMS, III, AMBER C. BRYANT
AND CHANCE W. LEWIS

27. EDUCATION, ECONOMICS & SEGREGATION IN BATON ROUGE

Embedded within the heart of Baton Rouge is a saleable level of civil unrest. Peering into the city from the lens of the national media, it would appear that the heavily segregated city is the result of poor race relations between the Black and White citizens. Upon further review, however, a number of factors have defined the fragile relationships, with one of them being inequitable school environments primarily resulting in low-achievement levels of African American students.

During the so-called post-racial Obama era, much attention is given to institutions in American society that continue to produce inequitable access to socioeconomic opportunities. Here, we discuss certain educational factors in the East Baton Rouge Parish over the last 15 years that have contributed to segregation, income inequality, and inept living conditions for Black citizens in Baton Rouge. We provide rational recommendations that can immediately impact and improve the educational conditions for the citizens of Baton Rouge.

A BRIEF HISTORY

Baton Rouge is the second largest city in the state of Louisiana with a population of over 225,000 following closely behind New Orleans' nearly 400,000 residents; the ethnic composition of Baton Rouge is 39% White, 55% Black or African American, and 3% Hispanic or Latino. Compared to New Orleans, within the last 50 years, Baton Rouge has experienced notably different political reform resulting in distinct structural differences between the two cities.

The city of Baton Rouge is a part of the East Baton Rouge Parish (EBRP) which is similar to what most cities would consider a county. Outside of differences in demographics, Baton Rouge also differs from New Orleans in the evolution of its school system; notably, it does not share the strong history of parochial schools as seen in New Orleans and Baton Rouge has not experienced New Orleans' history of gradual desegregation.

After the 1950's, New Orleans' African American population began to experience the benefits of increased economic mobility. Baton Rouge, an industrial neighbor of New Orleans, began to experience an increase in African American populations.

© KONINKLIJKE BRILL NV, LEIDEN, 2018 | DOI 10.1163/9789004378735_027

The increase in the Black population was accompanied by a decrease in the White population.

This phenomenon is known as *White Flight*. Baton Rouge is similar to other cities such as Detroit, Baltimore, St. Louis, Washington, D.C., during this period. It has been reported, based on census and population data, that for every Black family that moved into the city, approximately four White families moved out.

Due to the chronic economic and historic oppression of communities of color in America, Baton Rouge's influx of Black families from the 1950's–present and the simultaneous exodus of White residents resulted in a disproportionate economic distribution of wealth. Property-taxed based education systems as seen in Baton Rouge and most U.S. cities are vulnerable to demographic shifts and the economic conditions of their communities. America's sociopolitical history as well as the unique evolution of the city's region are both indicative of social conditions present today.

THE CURRENT STATE OF BATON ROUGE

Baton Rouge's current economic and divisive segregated condition is a derivative of the local policy and stance on education. Education has always been exclaimed as the vehicle which could remove the limitations of poverty, and propel anyone into their own American dream. For Blacks living in Baton Rouge, this dream has been unfulfilled with limited possibilities of change on the horizon.

As opportunities for economic growth in areas densely populated have dwindled for citizens of color other areas around Baton Rouge flourished. This phenomenon has created division within the city. Prime examples of this division are evident through the fight for equal education in Baton Rouge. Schools outside of the city have the luxury of drawing from a significant property tax base. Outside the city there is an abundance of homeowners. The lack of homeowners in EBRP, and the scarcity of businesses that are willing to build within the city has left EBRP with an income shortage.

As such, the school district is unable to provide an equitable schooling experience for students, particularly students in the lower socio-economic areas of the city and parish (county). This situation has served to create two realities; an increase in the number of students who graduate from high school, but are unable to attend a four-year university; and the creation of a low skilled, unprepared working class who must settle for low wage positions.

Furthermore, for those who are fortunate enough to excel in their academics and are accepted into Southern, LSU, or any other university, there are few incentives for them to return to an area which is void of employment opportunities for college graduates. Whereas in the previous decades, neighborhoods within the EBR parish (county) reflected a wide range of citizens who were college graduates, or gainfully employed skilled labors; now exists little, if any glimpse of hope as to how education can benefit someone in their community.

No Child Left Behind (NCLB) touted the creation of growth through increased accountability and standards, yet left school districts like EBRP exposed to further segregation. In 2002, as a response to increased accountability, Louisiana reclaimed several schools, in an effort to reform practice and improve student outcomes. In creating the Recovery School District (RSD), the Louisiana Department of Education relegated control of specific underperforming schools to charter organizations; RSD has struggled to reform its school into better learning environments, but have peeled away funding, talent, and resources from other schools in EBRP.

Another unintended event resulting from the creation of RSD are the initiatives from unincorporated parts of East Baton Rouge (Central and St. George) to create their own school districts, outside of the city limits of East Baton Rouge. In 2005, Central School District successfully partitioned from EBRP, creating a cultural divide between itself and EBRP in an effort increase academic outcomes for their students. The decision was favorable for the municipality of Center, as the Central School District propelled itself to become one of the leading school districts in academic achievement in Louisiana.

After unsuccessfully seeking their own school for two years, citizens of the upper-middle class unincorporated area of St. George pursued a similar path. While situation appears to resemble a move to gain control of schools in the area, underneath the surface it harkens memories of white flight. Successful incorporation would allow St. George to manage their own schools, comprised primarily of White students. In so doing, it would drastically reduce local and state funding for schools in EBR, predominantly made up of Black students. Though the initial effort to incorporate fell short in 2015, residents of St. George remain determined to advance this issue to ballot, increasing educational, economic, and racial tensions in Baton Rouge.

While it is important to extract historical patterns of disproportionality in Baton Rouge; the mere recognition of such patterns without practical solutions going forward are more damaging to future generations of Baton Rouge residents who seek to benefit from the local educational system. To aid educators, policymakers and politicians in their concerted effort to explore alternatives to improving the educational system, we have provided recommendations for educators. The remaining recommendations are applicable to policy makers and politicians.

Recommendation for Educators: Develop and Present a Plan for Educational Improvement to Policy Makers and Politicians

Provide evidence-based practices and professional development that might result in improved academic achievement for students in East Baton Rouge. This is an urgent call for educators in Baton Rouge and nationally who are on the front-lines to provide recommendations to policymakers, politicians and other stakeholders that can benefit students in low-performing schools in EBR. These recommendations should be implemented aggressively, meaning educators should formally present

113

these best practices to any stakeholder that have a vested interest in the educational system.

Presently, the state of Louisiana is at a loss in what works for urban schools in low-income areas. This appears evidenced by the example of transferring schools in EBR to the Recovery School District (RSD) and then back to the EBR school district without a formidable plan for improvement. To derive the most benefit for students, educators should provide an academic plan with funding provisions that are scalable to all schools to provide the support needed to improve academics.

Recommendations for Policy Makers and Politicians: Amend Funding Formula Policies for Schools

As it stands, the state and local funding formulas for low-performing urban schools that primarily serve African American youth in Baton Rouge are at best, a failure. These funding formulas have reverted the EBR school system into a separate and unequal system. A tour of low-performing and high-performing schools within the same school district clearly show the disparity in the funding formula. All residents and students are constituents and these policies should provide equal opportunity for educational and economic prosperity towards the American Dream.

To further explain why funding formulas should be revised – the EBR school system recently made a decision to renovate two high schools. The first, Robert E. Lee High School is a high-achieving school and second, Istrouma High School, is low-achieving. An investment of $56 million was granted for Robert E. Lee High School in comparison to a $15 million allocation for Istrouma High School.

This urgent call for politicians and policy makers to fixing these policies should be at the forefront of these political and policy discussions. Viable solutions to the educational system benefits students and their families; but such solutions also support the overall growth and vitality of the city of Baton Rouge and the parish (county) of East Baton Rouge.

Solutions should be feasible, measurable, and sustainable with intentional and deliberate action plans implemented at all levels. Academic progress should be tracked vigorously within schools and adjustments should be made both to school level (e.g., curricula and administration) and resources allocations (e.g., funding) to ensure and protect student academic growth.

CONCLUSION

An equitably educated Black body is necessary if East Baton Rouge seeks to illicit change in community relations between its citizens and its law enforcement members. A comprehensive approach to reforming schools that primarily educate African Americans would improve their educational and economic opportunities. Beyond that important outcome, it would also send a resounding message locally that all lives, regardless of color or creed, should be afforded the undeniable opportunity to access the American Dream.

It will take time for the effects of these changes to create a lasting impact; the benefits of reforming the curriculum and education funding formula far outweigh the negative perspectives and fallout that critics would attest to. All lives truly matter when all students and citizens are taught in schools and school systems that matter.

CLARICE THOMAS AND MARTHA DONOVAN

28. WHAT DOES IT MEAN TO BE UNITED?

Black death is the physical death that transpires at the hands of police. It is the death of citizenship, health, opportunity, and spirit. Black blood is spilled within numerous systems: education, healthcare, social service, and the criminal justice system. The U.S. Constitution ensures the strength of property rights, yet discriminatory laws and policies further the inequitable distribution of property and the favoring of White lives.

Despite gains in civil rights and the overturning of overtly racist laws, the systems were never redesigned to acknowledge the full citizenship of Black Americans. The Black body has never stopped being managed for compliance. Black men and women are appropriated for inexpensive labor. U.S. prisons represent major links in the chain of Black death. Schools rarely interrupt the cycle. They promote rote behavior and surface-level intellectual achievement in the face of accountability mandates. Education researchers whose work is driven by a need to create a more just and equitable world for Black students face a duty to forge alliances that desegregate intellectual communities create new paths forward.

Inspired by the relational space of narrative inquiry, two educational researchers, one Black and one White, forged a bridge to generate understanding of the reality of unequal schooling in the United States, to find common ground in their disparate narratives, and to imagine a safer future for Black lives. In this chapter, the authors' stories are told through a combination of commentary and italicized dialogue. Where dialogue is shared, the authors are identified as *CT* (Clarice Thomas) and *MD* (Martha Donovan).

The authors met at a coffee shop to talk through this project. This had to be a raw project, born from shared ideas. In their meetings, Clarice and Martha committed to learning from one another through bringing herself to the table talking directly about racialized differences they had lived throughout their lives. This took open-mindedness, strong listening, and acknowledging what each knew that the other did not know, as well as what they knew in common. They both opened up to try to say exactly what it was that they needed to discuss: Black life. White life. Their lives *as* Black and White. This work was founded in a critical race commitment both authors shared. Their talks ignited an action-oriented epistemic work, in-progress, and both the authors realized the blinding effect of their own color blindness.

But all their experiences are situated in an *active* history, a history built on internalized racial hierarchies that privileges Whiteness. Sharing their stories and coming to understand each other's experiences made them both angrier, but willing to forge new roads together in their research and teaching. Clarice reflected on their anger and noted, "When you think about it- in a fight- the action happens when you get mad. We just need to make sure our fights are proactive and not reactive."

UNITING OUR VOICES

To consider the possibility for a unified narrative, the two authors had to first question their separate narratives. What does it mean to be a Black woman in America? Are Black women's experiences the exact opposite of White women's? The divide between experiences, even looking specifically at education, tells a story of institutions functioning differently. What does it mean to be a White woman in America? What tropes of femininity and racial privilege have White women mastered at such young ages they are unaware of it? Do these tropes of privilege ensure that White women cannot understand the experiences of Black women? What does this mean when we seek unity to nurture Black lives?

CT: My teaching experiences were at several alternative education programs. In those spaces, I saw the damage of a broken system. My students understood the incarceration system's role in their lives more than the ideals of freedom and democracy, because those ideals didn't – and don't – apply to them.

As a teacher, Clarice was immersed in the school-prison nexus. She was responsible for empowering students with interrupted educations to complete high school. She saw what the cycle of racial segregation, income inequality, and behavioral discrimination in schooling, housing, and other social services often leads to. Her later immersion in research focused on refiguring the school to prison connection emerged from these experiences – both as a teacher, and as part of her community. Martha, as a White woman, came to research focused on Black lives through her experiences in educational policy studies. She was drawn to investigating the intersections of policy and social life; however, when she turned her attention to studying the impact of policy on teachers, she found that White bias in research has resulted in an education story that is always partial and sometimes false.

MD: The stories of Black schooling were either undermined by being subsumed in the "general story" from which they were historically excluded, or they are marginalized as a separate story *even since* the time that schooling experiences for Black students were supposedly no longer separate from White students. Yet as educators, we are responsible for all our students, which means we are all responsible for the inequities in school attainment and incarceration rates.

Clarice and Martha engaged in this shared space with the understanding that in order to make a difference in the lives of Black students, their differences, as well as their similarities, would need to be better understood. As teachers and researchers, they wanted their shared understandings to inform the greater community of educators. They imagined their process of radical sharing could enable them to interrupt the process in which Black children are targeted by school discipline policies, blamed for school failure, ushered into juvenile detention centers, and, ultimately, indicated for incarceration.

Given the numerous criminalized spaces that increase the incidence of Black death, Clarice and Martha's narratives ventured away from schooling and research to stories of interactions with law enforcement. In sharing their stories of the role of law enforcement in the perpetual over-punishing of Black bodies, they discovered very different understandings of how interactions with police officers transpired. They also discovered very similar understandings of how schooling for Black children too often includes discipline structures and teaching methods that metaphorically resemble those in the prison system.

CT: In my hometown, the police were always everywhere. It didn't matter where ... the suburbs or the city. They were everywhere, looking to pull drivers over, looking for warrants. I got pulled over ... I don't know how many times. Once I got pulled over because my graduation tassel was hanging from my rear-view mirror. Whenever they stopped us they would ask for everyone's ID and sometimes they'd ask the men to get out of the car. Black men in the presence of White officers were perceived as a threat, and they were handcuffed for "everyone's" safety.

MD: Whenever I've been pulled over they ask for the driver's ID. That's it. I've never had to get out of the car and I've never been with anyone who got handcuffed.

CT: So it's not standard for police to check everyone's ID in the car?

MD: No, I don't think so. At least, not for White people.

This conversation represents one of the many moments in their narrative sharing when Clarice and Martha's clearly illustrated separate and unequal systems. Symbolic integration efforts of the late twentieth century, most noticeably, school desegregation, not only failed to dismantle these systems, but resegregation of schools and persistent isolation of residential communities make it unlikely that Black and White people will even know what realities they face in these separate systems.

On the highest level of the U.S. government today, *blue* work is right while Black bodies are more often than not wrong. Black men and women are targeted by police and presumed guilty. Neither is ever really proven innocent. Debates about the innocence of Michael Brown, for example, turned relativist in White media: he was a thug, therefore not innocent, never mind his lack of weapon the night he was shot, or that use of force is only meant for when officers face an imminent threat. Michael Brown was threatening relative to his status as a young Black man. Black children in schools are held to strict standards of behavior, decorum, and achievement, and then punished, isolated, and/or restricted for behavior that falls out of line. However, given the strictness of the rules and standards to which the children are held, stepping out of line and facing the consequences happen as a matter of course.

MD: I'm sure I struggled to walk in perfect silent lines and comply all the time. But I have strong memories of teachers' eyes shifting to the Black children out of line. And I think it is harder for Black children now, amidst the demands of standards-based instruction, where everything is about preparing for tests, which may seem to have zero relevance to the daily lives they live and the futures they envision.

CT: I always knew as an African American my existence carried a different level of risk that my White woman counterparts may not experience. The risk is externalized as fear in simple actions throughout my day. I wear my research like armor; it has become all that I think, see, and breathe, but it is not protective. Every morning that armor feels heavy as I pull up to the car line to drop my African American sons off at their elementary school. I give them my words of advice, and disrobe my own protection in order to be theirs. I drive away with my fears and worry. I wonder, what challenges will they face today.

Educators must recognize the differences between how White and Black kids face the threat of punishment. Neither White children nor their teachers face discipline and punishment as Black children and teachers do. Black children's behavior is hyper-scrutinized, and their teachers are penalized when students do not succeed on standardized assessments. Black teachers have historically been fired en masse. An example seen in cases of closings of all-Black schools or with the repurposing of schools from public to charter, as in New Orleans in 2005. Black students are disproportionately removed from school and placed on a life course that may include incarceration.

The prevalence of punishment is a problem in Black spaces and the possibility of educational, spiritual, and physical death represents the other side of Black life. The school is a microcosm of the world at large, and a critical actor in the systemic demise. By inviting teachers and researchers to the epistemic work, may close the gaps between what is known and unknown, and promote pedagogical resistance in favor of equity.

Clarice learned at a young age that though she was considered smart, she would be frequently punished in school for failing to meet the expectations of conformity. Martha learned young that Black children were more likely to be penalized for infractions she herself also committed. Foucault theorized that the system was designed to imbue some bodies with value while stripping the dignity of citizenship from others.

The structure and function of the system can be learned, however, and in sharing narratives about structures that perpetuate inequities, educators can re-invigorate democratic schooling for social justice. In this process, researchers need to utilize their voices, pens, and platforms to create more just spaces. That space must include invitations to others; it must be accessible and lead to action at the most basic level:

personal relationships. In sharing their narratives, Clarice and Martha understood that their contemplation of their places in the school-prison nexus entailed risk. However, they understood that in order to imagine a future without Black death, their risks – as scholars and as persons – must be accepted. By engaging in uncompromising honesty about their experiences and searching for a unified narrative, they are proposing that new knowledge, and thus new possibilities for unity between Black and White people, can be born. With this unity, the cycle of control and punishment that permeates Black life can be broken.

JIE YU

29. WOUNDS AND BAND-AIDS IN
A DIVIDED SOCIETY

In the week before I began to write this chapter, President Trump signed an Executive Order entitled "Protecting the Nation from Foreign Terrorist Entry into the United States," which denied the entry of citizens from seven countries into the United States for 90 days. The seven predominantly Muslim countries were Iran, Iraq, Libya, Somalia, Sudan, Syria and Yemen. What surprised me then was a huge support of this immigrant ban from the Chinese immigrant community in the U.S.

Later I posted in one of my social media accounts: "Just want to remind the Chinese supporters of the new president along with his latest immigration ban policy that the first executive order banning immigrants only based upon nationality in the U.S. history is 'The Chinese Exclusion Act' signed into law by President Arthur in 1882." Quickly a comment was made to the post within only a few hours, "The Chinese Exclusion Act was fundamentally different; it was about jobs. Refugee ban is about national security."

After I replied that "I doubt both, for the former was much more than jobs while the latter cannot be justified for the sake of national security," the immediate response from this apparently Chinese supporter of both the president and his immigrant ban was, "Actually the Chinese Exclusion Act made exceptions for students and merchants. It only banned labourers. These are the people you look down upon anyway; they are like the Blacks and Mexicans today, so it's misleading to say the Chinese Exclusion Act affects people like us."

Several things stand out from the above comments upon my post. First, there is a clear and possibly wide divide between "us" and "them." As specified in the comments, *they* could be lower class Chinese "labourers" in history, and "the Blacks and Mexicans" in the contemporary society. On the other side of *them*, *we* have been the predominantly white Americans possibly along with "model minority" Asians. Here, social class and racial issues go hand in hand.

Second, such an apparent divide between "us" and "them" seems to place the two groups or even categories of people differently in a caste system of society. As suggested by the comments, they are the people we "look down upon." Last, since we and they are so different from each other in the social structure, we should not be concerned with possible consequences that affect *them* rather than *us*. In other words, we are not only different from but superior to them, so we do not need care about them. The core message is *their* lives do not matter, at least to *us,* in the divided society.

© KONINKLIJKE BRILL NV, LEIDEN, 2018 | DOI 10.1163/9789004378735_029

This divide between *them* and *us* reminds me of a familiar argument I hear almost every semester when teaching the Diversity and Multicultural course, a course required for all Education majors and minors in my department. When it comes to the discussion of racism and education in this class, some students, usually white, question, "When can we stop talking about colours or labelling people by colours? No matter what colours we are, we are essentially the same species of human being."

On the surface, it is true that all of us are human beings. Even the concept of race is not a real one, but a social product made by people. But what is often (un) consciously ignored by many people is that this artificial construct of "race" has real consequences for all of us, especially people of colour.

The name of this product is racism. Those different boxes of "races" were first created because of racism, the need to legally categorize people in a strictly-structured system for the sake of exploitation by certain groups people above others. Consequently, different life values are assigned to different groups or categories of people. It is not hard, then, to understand how comes the seemingly bold and arrogant statement, "the Blacks and Mexicans today" are "the people you look down upon."

As the values of *our* lives are greater than *theirs*, lives of people of colour, the divide between *us* and *them* becomes a wide gap that can be hardly crossed, separating *us* and *them* as two distinct and even hostile groups on two sides. Such a divide or gap inevitably causes wounds between the communities that are difficult to heal. The wounds cause everlasting pain for all, but especially for people of colour.

In the month after the release of the new immigrant ban, a racist incident occurred on the campus of a local college in my town. Someone put a big X crossing the word of "Black" in the title of an invited public talk to the college, "Black Lives Matter in the Age of Trump." Non-coincidentally, my students in the Diversity course this spring had an intense discussion regarding the Black Lives Matter and Blue Lives Matter movements.

In the discussion, students who called the supporters of Black Lives Matter *terrorists* questioned if it implied the lives of those who are not Black do not matter. Then I inserted another question: "Whose lives do you find more vulnerable in our society today?" I wanted to use this question to remind my students of the original initiatives of the movements. Black Lives Matter was not the belief that Black lives are more important than others but the opposite reality: that Black lives have been endangered and even threatened in this divided society.

The discussion of the two BLM movements was a tough and even disturbing one for my students. The discussion did, ultimately, allow them to see that the wounds cut by the divide between the communities are still bleeding under various Band-Aids, rather than healing or healed. Colour-blind liberalism might be one of the most convenient and effective Band-Aids used to cover the bleeding wounds.

Two of the typical colour-blind arguments are *everyone should be treated equally*, and let's *focus on human beings, not colours*. When my class discussed the *Fisher v. University of Texas at Austin* case this spring, the majority of the predominantly white class agreed that affirmative action in college and university admissions cannot be justified by either the slavery historically or contemporary underrepresentation of Black and Hispanic students in higher education. President Trump, coincidently, expressed his support for a merit-based immigration system when addressing Congress in February 2017, right before this class discussion upon affirmative action.

When students in my course argued that college and university admissions should be based on academic merit, without consideration of the factors that cannot be controlled by individual choices or efforts (i.e. race), I brought in the similar merit-based immigration system proposed by the president. One immediate response from the class was, "But the two systems are completely different." In the following deeper deconstruction of the two merit based systems, however, the students noticed a similar *survival of the fittest* core to both systems.

As the social Darwinism becomes self-evident in both merit based systems, one student shared his observation, "Oh, it's just like the American dream. It persuades people to work hard with the promise that they then will become successful. It thus also means if you fail, it's only because you aren't working hard enough. But, what if the system tricks you?" This interesting twist to the discussion made the students recognize the merit based rationale of "only the strong survive" is an ironic but brutal myth in an uneven playing field. But it is hard for the white community to acknowledge its privileges along with the disadvantages of people of colour as groups in a much bigger picture of the whole society. On the contrary, the supporters of colour-blind liberalism believe the society had made such great progress in the past in eliminating slavery and racism that we should be even more concerned today with "reverse" discriminations against whites.

Colour-blind liberalism denies how that long history of racism, including both institutional and individual racism, has shaped the current un-level playing field. It is also unwilling to admit that white privileges and disadvantages or discriminations against the people of colour coexist with each other – any change of the tilts in the uneven field will inevitably affect *all*. In this sense, colour-blind liberalism in a society where racism has been deeply entrenched is just another form of racism. Its critique of the playing of race card can be conveniently used as a Band-Aid to cover the wound without treating it.

The in-depth discussion of both questions, "Whose lives are more vulnerable?" and "Whose lives really matter?" is a good attempt to touch on and lift the Band-Aids for a critical comprehensive examination of the wounds. A careful and patient contextualized scan and understanding of the wounds is more important than immediate recommendations of treatments, especially as quick fixes to merely relieve wound pains.

Although the past presidential election was a struggling, even painful, experience for many people, including me, it had at least one good by-product: the large number of supporters along with the nationwide strong support received by the Trump campaign relentlessly lifted before the country the Band-Aids on the wounds in this divided society. Finally, we are disillusioned by a direct and clear view of the bleeding wounds while feeling the wound infections and pains.

Given that the treatment of the wounds requires the collaboration of all subsystems of the society, one suggestion I want to discuss briefly is to build organic *connections* between the divided *communities* through *conversations* for a genuine *care* of others.

For example, a genuine care toward others who are different from "us" seems to come as the last one, as the ultimate purpose and result of the first 3Cs, but that genuine care has to be cultivated earlier on to initiate conversations and connections between communities. At the end of each stage of the 4 Cs, not only the circle of care beyond us, but conversations and thus connections between divided communities, are widened. The result is not a simple increase of knowledge of others, but both enriched understanding of the otherness of *others* and critical reflections about *us*.

I want to end the chapter with a safety alert email I received from a contact group in my predominately white neighbourhood. The end of the email mentioned a piece of news of a young woman pushed by a Black man from a New York subway platform onto the tracks. My own Googling showed this accident on March 12, 2017 was that a woman fell to the tracks after she fainted on the platform. Now when I look at the news title in which each letter of the word, "FAINTING," was capitalized, it is shouting, "The wounds are still bleeding in this divided society." After the Band-Aids are off, it's time to heal wounds rather than relieve the pain.

AARON J. GRIFFEN

30. WHITE MATTERS

I remember the first time I was called *nigger.* I was six years old in Corpus Christi, Texas around 1980. I had been playing in a neighbour's yard. I do not clearly recall what action I committed to provoke such a reaction; nevertheless, "Get away from here, you nigger," still resonated. At the time, I did not recognize the word *nigger.* I had never heard *nigger* nor had I heard anyone in my family speak, *nigger*. I knew by the tone that *nigger* was negative and meant to illicit harm in some way.

So, in my six-year-old way, I repeated to the White girl with whom I was playing, "your daddy called me a nigger. He is a nigger!" Ironically, none of the predominantly Black and Hispanic children in the D.N. Leathers Housing Projects of Corpus Christi knew the word *nigger* either. Therefore, when the White girl stated, "Aaron called my daddy a nigger; it's going to be a fight," none of the children paid any attention to the word, *nigger,* but rather to the fight that was about to commence.

I never told my mother about that day, even when I recalled it years later. When asked about segregation she is reticent to recall experiencing any educational segregation. Interestingly, she does recall the time when she was a nurse, a little White girl spit in her face as my mother checked her vitals. Needless to say, Mommy would have been lynched had she lived in the South for the slap she handed that White girl.

THE UNITED STATES IS BLACK AND WHITE

The United States is *Black* and *White*, not by colour, not by race, but by simple concept. The concept of *Whiteness* did not begin with Jim Crow or slavery. The concept of Whiteness began when the ruling class began to grow in their concerns of a potential revolt akin to the French Revolution and that which resulted in the initial emigration to the New World.

The United States (U.S.) did not want a king's rule, setting in motion the idea that no religion or group would rule the new nation. When census data revealed that Africans were beginning to outnumber Europeans, however, something had to be done to maintain the *natural order*. At the same time as the transplantation of Africans to the New World, there was also an immigration of Eastern Europeans, not a part of the ruling class. Many of these individuals came as indentured servants, providing a service of seven years in exchange for transport to the U.S.

The ruling class, or the nobles, as they defined themselves, determined that to ensure the natural order they would devise a system where poor Europeans would

© KONINKLIJKE BRILL NV, LEIDEN, 2018 | DOI 10.1163/9789004378735_030

be taught that they were better than the African slave and the indentured Africans. They created a divide-and-conquer manifesto. That manifesto outlawed reading and writing for the Africans while promising land ownership and education to the poor Europeans.

For the poor Europeans, it was better to have more than Africans as opposed to have nothing and be equal to them. Despite the education system having been designed to relegate them factory workers and labourers for the nobles. This same perception was played out in the 2016 presidential election, where poor and rural Whites believed that their jobs had been taken by illegal immigrants and that to make *America Great Again*, they had to vote against their own interests in order to gain a higher status over African Americans and other racial groups.

The concept of *Whiteness* has been maintained. Poor and rural Whites voted for Trump knowing they might lose health care, but holding on to hope that they would be provided a step up for supporting their candidate. They failed to realize that in both the old America and the new America, poor Whites are *conceptually Black*. To be White, one has to own property and have higher education. Failure to attain both makes you Black – haves and have nots.

GUNS AND BUTTER

To fully understand the concepts of *Whiteness* and *Blackness* one must recognize the difference between *guns* and *butter*. Guns represent Whiteness. Butter represents Blackness. Guns are items that appreciate. They grow in value like fine art, real estate, and assets. They appreciate in monetary value over time, producing wealth for their owners. Owners polish their guns regularly. They invest. They use the best polish available: Goldman Sachs, Century 21, and Charles Schwab.

The polish ensures the value of their investments grows. If there is a dip, Wells Fargo, Chase, and Uncle Sam come to bail them out. Access to guns, however, is limited to those who can attain one via sound investment in the right gun stores – through quality education and family legacy. Pulling yourself up by your bootstraps is the common butter mantra from the top 1 percent of the country who achieved their guns, they believe, through the hard work of their family.

For those who do not have a family legacy via insurance, trusts, or the resources to gain an education to teach us about guns, we are fed butter. Butter represents all that depreciates, loses value. These are cars, clothes, entertainment, and credit cards. Gun owners feed us butter because that is how they maintain their guns. We accept this butter because butter makes everything taste better. The advertisements tell us what cars to buy, what shoes to purchase, and the next trip to take. The gun owners feed us butter because they prey on our emotions and psychological dispositions. We are uncomfortable and butter makes things better.

While the gun owners polish their guns, they remain skinny and hungry. They feed us the butter that makes us fat, lazy, and lethargic. While we get all our fill of tasty butter, the gun owners prey on our laziness and feed themselves with more guns that they purchase from the revenue of butter they fed us. Our butter tasting makes us an asset to the gun owners.

All who own guns are *White*. All who own butter are *Black*. Regardless of race, colour, or ethnicity. When you start gaining access and owning guns, you become White. However, gun owners do not want too many Blacks suddenly becoming White. It challenges their power and position in the United States and that of their heirs.

LGBTQ IS THE NEW BLACK

Being Black was never a problem so long as African Americans were the only Blacks. Even if a few Mexican Americans, Hispanics, and Asians were thrown in, there was no problem. The problem of *Blackness* became an issue for other groups as soon as they began to be marginalized like other Black groups.

With family rights not afforded to LGBTQ community members, the right to adopt became a question along with the right to marry. LGBTQ members suddenly felt the sting of Blackness. What the LGBTQ feels/felt is akin to how African Americans have felt since before the Declaration of Independence was scripted.

Africans could not marry without consent of their owners. LGBTQ members could not marry without consent of the government. If they did marry, they could be split, as their marriage was not recognized. Once LGBTQ member's marriage was not recognized in all states. Now that the Supreme Court recognizes gay marriage, the sting has subsided. Yet, the scars remain as new legislation is being introduced which allows employers to discriminate against those who are in gay marriages and relationships.

Voting rights were not initially extended to African Americans, nor were the rights to own property or gain an education. Like Palestinians in Israel, African Americans at one time were destined forever to be conceptually Black – a permanent minority with questionable political power. The Civil Rights Act and Affirmative Action, however, has changes our fate as a people. We could achieve higher education and buy property – conceptually White. With some of these rights being taken away or not afforded to the LGBTQ community, they are now the new Black.

The sting of this reality resulted in protests akin to the Civil Rights protests. Conceptually, White LGBTQ members benefited from Affirmative Action and the Civil Rights Act, so there was no reason to comment on the plight of African American people or others who were conceptually Black. Now that there is a roll back in the nation to include the LGBTQ, cries are loud and an intersection of all groups is being discussed. The intersection was already there, but their Whiteness, like those of the poor Europeans of the New World, blinded their reality. They would rather be a step above Black versus being seen as Black. Now they're Black like me.

BLACK LIKE ME

The new Blackness also extends to Muslims and Mexican Americans. The signing of the Executive Orders to build a wall between the United States and Mexico and immigration bans 1.0 and 2.0 immigration results in the new Blackness of Middle Eastern and North East African people. The mass deportations of groups have taken some Blackness of African Americans away, transferring it to other groups.

Like the LGBTQ community, many Muslim Americans did not question or comment on the Blackness of African Americans. They were perceived as White because they owned property and had higher education. Muslim Americans became synonymous with gas stations, while Asian Americans – Koreans, Chinese, and Japanese – are synonymous with nail salons and dry cleaners.

When the Executive Orders began hurting travel and challenging the immigration status of these groups, there was an outcry of support. The immigration status of Africans was never a question during slavery nor their citizenship and the right to vote. Suddenly, being Black is not good enough for these groups. The bad news is those that own the guns are already spreading the butter to these groups. If you are from Saudi Arabia or from United Arab Emirates, you are safe. This is because the Whiteness of those nations is conceptualized. Their guns are in good hands with Trump State.

CONCLUDING THOUGHT ON WHITE MATTERS

In the United States of America, *Whiteness* is all that matters. The more White you are, the better. Our nation is so egotistically White that we call ourselves Americans despite sharing North America with two other countries. Because our country owns the most guns, the others are not allowed to call themselves Americans. They are Canadians and Mexicans. They are conceptually Black.

Moving forward, we should flip the gun and butter game. We should focus on buying up property and gaining our education. Become a part of the system to change the system. Become conceptually White. In becoming apart of the system to change the system, conceptually Black people can begin to change the narrative and the definition that defines what it is to be American.

When people yell that America is a White man's country, we should no longer disagree. America is a White man's country – our conceptually White country. As we all move closer to conceptual Whiteness, its very definition becomes blurred. No more conceptual Whiteness or conceptual Blackness because we all fit the one description.

Many who yell, "America is a White man's country" are not actually White, they are conceptually Black. They spew the rhetoric of those who want to maintain the separation of groups so that one conceptually, socially and economically remains above all others. They simply do not have the education to recognize that they two are one of the "other" groups. Their White matters are hidden in this chapter.

www.ingramcontent.com/pod-product-compliance
Lightning Source LLC
Chambersburg PA
CBHW030654270326
41929CB00007B/355